Perfect Cholesterol In Just 3 Weeks (Without Drugs!)

Perfect Cholesterol
In Just 3 Weeks
(without drugs!)

<u>The</u> Answer to High Cholesterol

David M. Vitko, D.C.

Rock Solid Health Solutions, Inc.
P.O Box 5
Columbiana, Ohio 44408

A Rock Solid Health Solutions Book
Published by Rock Solid Health Solutions, Inc.

Rock Solid Health Solutions®, is a registered trademark. All rights reserved. This trademark may not be used in any form without express written consent. For information, please contact Rock Solid Health Solutions, Inc. at P.O. Box 5, Columbiana, Ohio 44408. Web address: concretehealth.com   Phone: Toll Free 1-877-418-3324

Printed in the United States of America

Text editing by Daniel M. Votaw
Jacket design by Design Studio

Publisher's Cataloging-in-Publication Data

Vitko, David M.
  Perfect Cholesterol In Just 3 Weeks (without drugs!)/David M. Vitko
  p.   cm.

ISBN 0-9762698-0-5
       1.   Lowering Cholesterol
       2.   Diet - Health
       3.   Heart Disease - Prevention
       4.   Self-Care

Library of Congress Control Number: 2004097562

Dedication

This book is dedicated to my loving wife Denise, the source of my strength and direction. And to my incredible kids, Kelly and David, who give me great pride and joy.

It is also for my parents who instilled into me, a strong sense of right and wrong. They also provided me with a huge appreciation for the value of common sense.

This book is written in the sincere hope that my children, your children, and one day their children, might enjoy the incredible health that we all were cheated out of, so far.

Contents

Warning and Disclaimer

Foreword

Yes, you *can* have perfect cholesterol! You can totally conquer your cholesterol problem without drugs. And, best of all, you will also gain incredible control over every minute aspect of your health.

What? You say that your cholesterol is fine? Your doctor said it was OK? Think again. Some of the world's most forward thinking experts may disagree with your doctor over what constitutes good cholesterol levels. Today, acceptable blood cholesterol levels are dictated by what is attainable with the use of prescription drugs. These standards fail to consider the naturally low cholesterol levels of vibrantly healthy cultures outside the United States.

Prescription drugs often influence the standards doctors use to determine whether or not blood work is considered acceptable. Yet, living within these standards may do little to promote optimum health.

One sign that the drug companies recognize this problem is reflected in the new push for even lower total cholesterol levels and increased HDL levels. This of course, will be accomplished through the introduction of new, stronger drugs. New drugs mean longer patent protection and huge profits (from you). Of course stronger drugs also means more potential side effects.

It is time for Americans to wake up!

Merely living as you please, while using medications to artificially manipulate blood chemistries that only provide the illusion of health, is obviously not the answer to our modern health dilemma.

Stop funding drug makers' lavish lifestyles with your hard-earned cash. *You* should enjoy the fruits of your labor, not some fat cat pharmaceutical executive. Did you work your tail off all these years just to hand all of your assets over to someone else? It's time to take back your health independence from the drug bosses, doctors, and nursing homes. *It's time for a real health revolution!*

Health is that one possession we must learn to treasure most. Your health is entirely your own. The government cannot tax it. (At least they haven't figured out yet how to tax it.) It is our most valuable possession. Yet, as many Americans are about to enter their "golden years" health seems to slip away quickly, without warning. The truth is that throughout our lives we squander our health gradually.

The reason for this travesty may seem too complicated for simplification. It is not.

By the time you finish this book, you will have one major question in your mind. Do the experts really not understand the simple origins of sickness and its root in our diet, or do they simply choose to ignore it for financial gain? In fact, they are all just part of a very big self-propagating money machine. Widespread application of the knowledge I share here would bring that big machine to a screeching halt. This obviously would be to the financial detriment of some very big players in the health game. Ironically, by continuing to support a failed system of health simply to maintain profitability, they sacrifice their own health as well as that of their loved ones.

Health care leaders would have us believe that health is at least partially outside of our control. You see, if you believe that you have little control over your health, you are forced to depend upon others for advice, direction, and leadership. This is how the "health bosses" maintain control over your health, your life, and, therefore, your pocketbook.

I fully understand the process by which we gradually lose our health. And you can too. The answer is in this book.

The good news is that there is no reason we must lose our health as we age. Good health is free for the taking. No one can keep you from it if you really want it. All that is required is a different way of thinking. Modern medicine has professed to have the answers to our health problems for the past 100 years. Yet, as you and I look around it seems clear that we have not reduced cancer rates, and have actually seen the numbers of heart attacks and strokes skyrocket in recent years. All of our lives have been touched by these problems. We have invested in the slash and burn method of health for long enough! It's time to open your eyes and see the truth.

In order for you to begin to enjoy total health, a change in attitude is needed. In speaking to patients over the years about health, there is one common denominator that I have noticed. And, it seems to be a prevalent attitude in our society. We are a society of whiners. That's right. Everyone has some kind of excuse about why they cannot adopt a healthy lifestyle. We choose not to accept responsibility for anything, including our most valuable asset, health. This attitude is the only thing holding America back from becoming the healthiest nation on earth. It is also the one thing that stands between you and supreme health.

We can no longer afford to wait for a knight in shining armor to arrive on a white horse (or in a white coat) to save us from our own poor health habits. The time is now. The answer is in your hands.

Learn to take responsibility for you own health.

As you will see, this requires a giant leap in faith, but the benefits are always commensurate with the effort. If you are tired of being a puppet to drug companies, insurance companies, nursing homes, and the government, this is your chance to take back your life. Imagine how wonderful life would be if you did not have to take any medications. Oh, how glorious the feeling to know that your future could include long relaxing walks on the beach rather than confinement in a nursing home until death. Dependence upon the government for medical care through Medicare could be a laughing matter if you so choose.

Yes, you can have perfect cholesterol. And you can also have impeccable health as a bonus. Find out how great life can be simply by reading and applying the principles in this book. The possibilities for improved health are infinite.

Preface

"No one should be forced to depend upon drugs to control their cholesterol."

This book has 4 reasons for being:

- First, to prove beyond all doubt that it is imperative for *everyone* to begin reducing cholesterol immediately! Every day that you live with total cholesterol over 160 mg/dl, your health is eroding. If you do not know your current cholesterol level, find out quickly. The length and quality of your life depends, to a very great extent, upon fixing the cholesterol problem! The information in this book will launch your understanding of cholesterol to a level that is light-years ahead of most doctors.

- Second, to demonstrate how high cholesterol contributes heavily to many health problems in addition to that with which we are most familiar, heart attack and stroke. High blood pressure, Alzheimer's disease, Parkinson's disease, arthritis, failing vision, hearing difficulties, hair loss, osteoporosis, and even back pain are but a few of the symptoms which reflect metabolic problems involving high cholesterol. Few doctors understand this important relationship, but you soon will.

- Third, to show why medications are not the correct answer to high cholesterol. The drug approach to high cholesterol is incredibly costly. This is hardly debatable. But the cost may go much farther than money. Many people have experienced significant health-damaging side effects from taking these drugs, for even a short time. The long-term effects are anyone's guess at this point. And worst of all, once you have started on cholesterol drugs, there are substantial risks to your health if you stop taking them.

- Lastly, to provide *the* simple answer to high cholesterol, as well as many seemingly unrelated diseases that are directly or indirectly connected to it. Not only can your cholesterol become normal, but health beyond your wildest dreams will be the welcome result! The return of youthful vigor is rule, rather than the exception.

We live in a society with strange ideas about health. The best that can be said about our health care system in this wonderful United States of America is that confusion and misdirection must be the goal. It is a system that ignores an abundance of critical information, which could free everyone from the burdens of illness. Yet, our health leadership clings to an inferior and outdated approach to health.

The status quo is greedily protected. Profits rule. Shame on those who ignore or even suppress life-saving information while propagating half-truths and endless hope as a means of selling high-cost, high-tech cures to a desperate people. Under this system millions of innocent people suffer needlessly every day. This sad situation exists in our beloved country, which possesses all the necessary resources to be the healthiest civilization in the history of the world.

We should be leading the world to infallible health. Our refusal to do so represents the most shameful inheritance we pass on to our children; our gift to future generations is an unstable economy based largely upon providing care to an increasing population of unfortunate souls who are unable to care for themselves.

American health care is overflowing with innocent victims. This book is meant to free those who are held captive by a costly and inefficient system. It is inspired by millions of children who suffer needlessly with childhood illnesses. I am driven by the thought of middle-aged folks discovering their own mortality by the onset of "the diseases of aging", a false premise. Lastly, it is for the elderly who worked a lifetime to get ahead, only to hand over every last cent of their life savings to the "sellers of health". It is a desperate yet always futile quest to purchase health in a bottle. For them, life ends when they enter the nursing home. For the pharmaceutical companies, physicians, and nursing home owners, this is when things really become lucrative. There is nothing like a captive audience to propel profits through the roof.

I have witnessed first-hand, the pain and suffering which accompanies sickness and infirmity. Few of us have been spared this experience. This book is written with heavy-hearted compassion for those who suffer needlessly. They are victims, for the most part, of complacency. This book is also written with empathy for doctors, nurses, and all health care workers. My hope is that they can overlook the necessary criticism herein, to also benefit from the health building information in this book. I find no fault with individual health professionals, except that few of them exemplify health. The real limitations fall on the professions and their business practices.

I believe that if today's health-care professionals could see the way to realistically improve their own health, they could accelerate a grass-roots health revolution that would catapult American health care to new heights. Leading by example is a potent tool to create change.

Traditional health care workers have been taught to believe that their work represents the best health care available. With all due respect, nothing could be further from the truth. Their application of accepted high-tech medical wisdom is valuable in its own way, no doubt. Not withstanding the work of trauma specialists, medicine's miraculous works pale in comparison to those nature provides for everyone who follows her unwritten rules. And, with each new high-tech discovery, drug, or surgical procedure, modern health care leaders draw an unsuspecting public further from the real truth about health.

During my years in the darkness of errant living, I have benefited greatly by the care of dedicated medical professionals. I personally am forever indebted to them for saving me from my own bad habits. Many are incredibly devoted to serving the hoards of suffering masses bent on self-destruction. How can one see and not appreciate the efforts they put forth to help us in our hour of need?

Yet, despite the well-publicized miracles, these medical professionals must feel a deep sense of frustration with their limitations. Regardless of their numerous, valiant efforts, they work with human bodies whose ability to heal is limited by the unwritten "Laws of Nature". A lifetime of living in a haphazard manner in which these indelible laws are broken on a daily basis, profoundly limits any effort to correct the resulting breakdown.

Powerful drugs and heroic surgery offer quick, temporary answers to patients' discomfort. They help to relieve symptoms by artificially interfering with errant molecular reactions caused by self-inflicted chemical imbalances. Drugs create a false sense of security by temporarily relieving symptoms.

"By its very nature, modern medicine propagates chronic disease and suffering."

Unsuspecting masses of the medically "cured" go about

their lives seemingly relieved of disease. There is no perceived need for further intervention. Modern medicine has an answer for each illness that strikes! Right? This is certainly what we have been taught from our youth up through old age. We know this to be the best that health care has to offer. This way of thinking seems beyond reproach. The consistent marketing drumbeat of the pharmaceutical giants has made it part of a larger social consciousness. For decades we have been saturated with half-truths too complicated for most people to see through. *The most destructive of these is that an absence of symptoms denotes health.*

Yet, beneath the façade of symptom-less health, all is not well. Abnormal processes fester deep within the cellular recesses of the body, despite your doctor's assurance that "you are healthy." Chemical imbalances for which no medical test has yet been designed to detect go unnoticed. These precursors of disease accumulate gradually, without notice. They quietly wait for the day our body's defenses are weakened to a vulnerable point. Then, and only then, they attack! Time, wrong living, and negative daily habits accumulate to the point at which the body loses command of cellular processes to "disease." At this point, even the best medical treatment can often do little to restore health. Acute illness, chronic and sometimes incurable disease, is the result.

Modern high-tech medicine places total emphasis on the treatment of disease with drugs and surgery. It is the definition of a "crisis care" model of health care. There are huge profits in this method. Prevention has been given secondary consideration. Efforts to promote prevention by modern medicine must necessarily include the use of potentially dangerous drugs. This approach to health is expensive, short sighted, and quite possibly the cause of a great deal of pain and chronic disease. Sickness is accepted and unwittingly fostered by this shallow view of health.

Little Prevention/Modern Medicine's Fault?

Modern medicine should not be held accountable for their reluctance to promote preventative lifestyles. They are, after all, experts in emergency treatment of sickness. They are disease specialists. Their education is complicated. It follows that their every day practice would also be complicated.

However, having the knowledge that as a profession, they have little inclination toward natural, self-health promotion should make us take pause. Modern medicine is the self-anointed guardian of our health. As a profession they have dictated health policy to us all for a very long time. I assert that this is wrong.

The medical profession should be given full authority over only that segment of health care they know the most about, treatment of disease. It is inherently wrong for a profession that makes its tremendous profits from sickness, to be in charge of teaching the public to be well. Where is the incentive for success? This would be the equivalent of putting politicians or the IRS in charge of teaching taxpayers how best to minimize their taxes.

The logical approach, providing that our goal is to create a truly healthy society, would be to develop an entirely new profession from willing practitioners of various health fields. Teach them the fundamentals of a healthy diet and lifestyle. Secure a commitment from them to live that lifestyle, to be a beacon of light for those less knowledgeable. Most importantly, develop a structure of practice that can be integrated with the old crisis care physicians to help patients move away from a drug based existence to a higher level of health. These practitioners should be the most highly rewarded of all physicians so that the profession could draw the best minds.

This brief description would be a vast improvement over the current crisis care model we presently depend upon for health care. It would end the stranglehold that the drug and insurance companies, as well as the nursing homes, have on our economy. This doesn't have to be just a dream.

The Narrow Path to Real Health

There is a better way to live than to depend upon crisis-oriented health care. All disease can be prevented if the *correct path* is followed. It is the sincere desire of this author to introduce others to this path to supreme health. Not only is disease avoidable, amazingly vibrant health is the **guaranteed result** of following this path.

It is simple in concept, yet even those who fully understand it often have trouble following it. The difficulty lies not in understanding or even accepting the concept, but rather in the application of this knowledge within this complex world, full of temptations and false beliefs, that is the greatest challenge. There are many pitfalls along the way. For those strong-willed individuals who persist, working daily to follow this straight and narrow path, anything is possible. Perfect health is the reward.

"Small is the gate and narrow the road that leads to life, and only a few find it."

Matthew 7:14

Be forewarned, there are many who would cherish the failure of your effort to become independently healthy. They will try to lure you from the path with half-truths and impossible promises. This deception is most often caused by their own misunderstanding and refusal to give up ingrained belief systems than from bad intentions. With regard to health issues, confusing information is used to reinforce an attitude of, "Oh, why bother? It's too difficult." Do not succumb to these lies. Know that there is only one way to true health. It requires effort.

Sickness is sometimes complicated. I concede this point. When sickness occurs it may require that you consult a doctor. But *health* is not difficult! There is a path, which automatically leads to good health. The longer you follow the path, the easier it is to recognize false concepts of health. Learn to follow this path and you can laugh with me at those who would sell you pills and potions as a means to becoming "healthy". It is utter nonsense!

There is no question that we are dealing here with deeply ingrained beliefs about health and disease. It is never easy to buck the system. I only ask that you as the reader approach the information I offer here with an open mind. In exchange, I promise that everything to follow is scientifically based and accurate. Some facts come from the research community, dug out of reputable sources like the National Library of Medicine. Others have been garnered from my own observations. If something represents my opinion without substantial scientific "proof" supporting it, I will say so.

At the end of this book you will find a list of many of the sources I study to develop a better understanding of health. I encourage you to become a student of health by both observing and recording your own health changes as related to diet, and by reading and studying from the sources I provide.

It should be obvious to you by now that science does not always represent the truth. Scientific studies come in many sizes, shapes, and colors. Much of today's science has been manipulated to fill a need for documenting the value of a new drug or other potentially profitable product. One clue of the value of a study is who paid for it. Unfortunately, this information is often hidden from public view.

This is not real science and should be scrutinized closely. Whatever science has to say about any given subject is often not really all that important. Truth does not change simply by the whims of man. Only the perception of truth can be altered.

With regard to health, truth is self-evident. Only patience and honest observation are required to discover the real truth. This requires no advanced college degree or superior intelligence. Simple common sense can go a long way in revealing the most important health information ever discovered. Pay attention and you will learn.

Chapter I
Why Everyone Must Reduce Cholesterol Now!

Most of us are painfully aware of the need to keep our total cholesterol under 200 mg/dl. Television, print advertising, news stories, and trips to the doctor have combined to saturate our lives with cholesterol facts. We are constantly being reminded that at levels above 200 mg/dl, cholesterol builds up inside our arteries. As blood vessels narrow, blood flow to vital organs, especially the heart, is reduced. This health issue is so important, negatively affecting so many people, that even the United States government has become involved. (What don't they try to control?) Unfortunately, our political leaders have provided little in the way of real guidance here. This health problem continues to cause millions of premature deaths and disability in our society.

The National Cholesterol Education Program (NCEP) is the federal government's attempt to inform the public about the latest cholesterol facts. The website can be found at www.nhlbi.nih.gov/chd/. It offers advice on diet and the use of medications to reduce and control cholesterol. If you do not have a computer, you can request related information by contacting the American Heart Association at 1-800-242-8721, or the American Stroke Association at 1-888-478-7653. You should be aware, however, studies have suggested that the diet recommended by these experts falls short of what is necessary to reduce cholesterol to optimum levels. My personal experience has demonstrated the same. Your doctor, based on his own experiences, would probably agree as well.

In his book *Reversing Heart Disease*, Dr. Dean Ornish says of patients on a 30% fat diet, such as that recommended by the American Heart Association, "the majority of these patients got worse, not better," referring to their battle with coronary heart disease.

The Problem with Cholesterol

First, you must know that cholesterol in appropriate proportions in our body is not our enemy. As a matter of fact, cholesterol is an incredibly important and versatile substance without which we could not survive.

Cholesterol is usually described as a waxy, fatty substance. It is both consumed in our diet and produced by the liver. Without cholesterol we could not live. However, we do not need to consume it. Our body produces all the cholesterol it needs. As a matter of fact, any cholesterol that is consumed must be processed by the body and disposed of, mostly through the gall bladder. This places an extra burden on the body.

Excess consumption of cholesterol or saturated fats tends to cause an accumulation of cholesterol in the blood stream. This is where the problems begin.

Cholesterol buildup, or plaque, which accumulates in our arteries, slows blood flow by narrowing the inside diameter of the vessel. That is the opening through which blood flows. At its worst, it can totally block the vessel causing blood flow to halt. This frequently causes a heart attack or stroke, depending on where the blockage occurs. Blockage in one of the coronary arteries, which brings blood to the heart, causes a heart attack. When blockage occurs in one of the many blood vessels supplying the brain, a stroke ensues. The extent of the injury you suffer depends upon which artery is blocked, and which part of the heart or brain is damaged.

The buildup of cholesterol in our arteries begins in our youth. By the time many of us have reached our 30s, it has progressed to a dangerous point. One need only to read the obituaries regularly to become painfully aware of the number of people dying in their 30s and 40s of heart attack or stroke.

It is my opinion that cholesterol is often involved in the sudden death of young athletes. It was once thought that exercise alone was enough to protect against heart attack caused by a less than optimal diet. The occasional death of a highly trained marathon runner demonstrates the fallacy of this attitude. *The recent death of a friend who was an avid runner drove this point home for me.* Exercise at any level should not be interpreted as a license to eat excessively or even incorrectly. You will see that elevated cholesterol levels in the blood place everyone at increased risk of early death, including young athletes.

This then extends the danger of elevated cholesterol levels to teenagers and young adults. Once you understand how cholesterol affects the blood, you will agree that no one, regardless of age, is safe from its risks.

For those who survive youth, the buildup of cholesterol continues to accumulate in the arteries gradually. Although older folks may have eluded an early death by heart attack, few will be spared the suffering caused by living with elevated cholesterol. The more cholesterol you have in your blood, the faster this blockage of the arteries progresses. Reducing cholesterol levels in your blood slows the speed at which this process takes place. It also reduces other related degenerative effects on your body.

By reducing cholesterol levels below a certain threshold, this buildup process can be halted, and even reversed! Dr. Ornish has demonstrated conclusively how simple changes in lifestyle can affect circulation to the heart. Reducing plaque by consuming a very low fat diet coupled with minimal exercise has been proved. What keeps us from making the necessary changes in our diet and lifestyle so that we can benefit from this knowledge?

Proof Positive

Evidence supporting the role of cholesterol in the buildup of plaque in the arteries could hardly be stronger or more convincing. Studies of monkeys have demonstrated that cholesterol is a major culprit in the accumulation of plaque in the arteries. (Like it or not, the physiological dietary needs of these animals are very close to the dietary needs of humans.) In one controlled study as reported in the Merck Manual, considered to be the authority on human disease, monkeys began to develop cholesterol buildup inside artery walls ***within just two weeks*** of the establishment of elevated cholesterol in the blood. How much more convincing do you need? There are many, many more studies that cement the relationship between elevated cholesterol in the blood and increased levels of disease.

I have heard the argument that those are animals and not humans. To this I say, "Bull!" If we were comparing ourselves to cows, which are ruminants (grazers), I would agree. Or, if the comparison were made to a true carnivore, such as the cat, that too would be a poor choice. But the fact is that apes are omnivores (though mostly fruit eaters), just like we are. They are designed physiologically, to thrive on a plant-based diet, just like we are. When apes are regularly fed cholesterol-elevating foods like meat, the result is circulatory compromise, just like we humans experience.

I can understand that there may be differences in specific chemical reactions between apes and man. These often show up in drug testing. But truth be known, drugs frequently have very different reactions from one *human being* to another. Despite the pharmaceutical industry's claims to the contrary, drug testing on apes has proved to be less valuable in many instances than researchers would like. How many times have we seen a drug approved by the FDA, then pulled from the shelf a short time later because it is killing humans en mass?

Many of these dangerous pharmaceuticals were tested extensively on animals and found to be "safe." But these experiments look at specific reactions of drugs on a given system. Something is missing from this approach. There are too many variables for this to ever be totally reliable.

I offer the fact that some humans can use one prescription drug liberally, while the same medicine might kill the next person. There is often no way of accurately predicting who can and cannot safely take any given drug. This demonstrates, at the very least, that all drugs are inherently dangerous and should be avoided if possible!

There are always possible interactions between multiple drugs taken in combination. The more drugs you take, the greater the chance of adverse short or long-term reactions. Even some foods that are consumed with a drug can cause harmful chemical interactions. This should give us all cause for concern. Why would anyone want to complicate his or her health picture that much if it is not necessary?

Within similar physiological systems, however, comparisons of dietary influences on the function of the body can be made with animals. By comparing anatomical features for instance, realistic comparisons of function can be made. Similarities in tooth structure, length of the digestive system, digestive processes, amounts and characteristics of digestive enzymes, and observations of natural diet make the comparison of ape and man of obvious value in cholesterol metabolism.

That which causes elevated cholesterol in apes also causes a comparable rise in man's cholesterol. This obvious relationship was one factor that helped me to make changes in my own diet in order to lower my cholesterol. The results were incredible. This lends support to my contention that we should look to our counterparts in nature to help us understand which dietary habits man's "superior intelligence" has caused us to forget. It helps us to understand what man's optimal diet should probably look like. When we begin to shun modern dietary practices and adopt a corrected or at least significantly improved diet, most chronic diseases will cease to exist.

By the way, I am opposed to the use of animals for research. It is my belief that if we all ate the foods that we are designed to eat, and couple this with a moderately active lifestyle, all human sickness would become negligible. Therefore, there would be little need for drugs to treat disease. And animal research would no longer be necessary.

I do not support any animal rights organizations, though I do sympathize with the animals' needless suffering. Animal research appears to me to be driven by greed and a misguided belief in a false system of health. It is often disguised as compassion for human suffering.

Drug companies are greedy for profits. The government is greedy for control. We are greedy for cures that will allow us to pursue our gluttonous lifestyle and still enjoy "good" health. It may be time for each of us to step back and take a long, hard look at our selfish values, especially as they relate to the other creatures of this world.

There are numerous human population based studies, which cement the connection between cholesterol and health. These studies are overwhelmingly convincing. In short they demonstrate the direct relationship between elevated cholesterol and an increased incidence of disease.

Few of us ever get to see this evidence in a meaningful form. Most of it is too complicated, never really reaching a useful conclusion. If it were organized and presented to the masses in an understandable way, it could be easily applied to lifestyle modification. Americans would quickly become the healthiest civilization the world has ever known.

Unfortunately, there is never enough data to convince the research community of anything. It is a self-propagating monster, often unable or unwilling to put valuable information into a form the average person can use (unless of course it helps them sell a new drug). Have you ever noticed that science is very good at offering eternal hope? Real solutions seem few and far between.

Wasted Money, Time, and Lives

I once wrote a letter to a man who donated millions of dollars to research a genetic cure for cancer. I believe there was a significant cancer case in his family, and this is what spurred him to do such a ridiculous thing. In my letter, I explained that the cause for most cancers had been known for a very long time. The cause was incorrect diet causing genetic mutations in the cells. I further explained that genetic research was just "pie in the sky" from which no effective treatment could result.

To my surprise, I received a letter back from one of the lead researchers at his institute. He patronized me by saying that I obviously had given this a lot of thought. He acknowledged that nutrition was an overwhelming factor in cancer, but that their institute had already committed millions of dollars towards finding a genetic cure. Too bad the rich folks in the world don't understand how their hard-earned money is being wasted by needless research that will never produce a "cure". If they did, perhaps they would invest their money on the one thing that would make real changes in the world's health, at a fraction of the price.

The real answer of course, is in educating the public about the effects of food on our health. I truly believe that when people *know with certainty* that certain foods lead to cancer and death, while others lead to supreme health, they will eventually learn to choose wisely.

Chapter II

Medical Approach to Cholesterol

We are now going to look at the modern medical approach to the problem of elevated cholesterol. Keep in mind that this mimics the views and treatment outcomes doctors have for other "disease processes" in the human body.

Medical practice treats elevated cholesterol as a disease. It is not a disease. **High cholesterol is no more than your body's adaptation to improper diet.** To understand the medical approach to this and many similar physiological alterations medical practice incorrectly treats as disease processes, explore the following thoughts. Let's start out with an analogy and a little quiz.

Let's say that you bought a new car. It's a beauty! You bargained the price down and got what you feel is a fantastic deal. This is good because you are basically a tight wad and don't want to give anyone the pleasure of thinking they made a buck off of you.

Being thrifty, you reason that over the life of the car,

estimated at ten years, a lot of money could be saved by buying the cheapest gas. Besides, this cheap gas station is right next to the fast food joint you eat at every day. It has really great bargains on burgers and fries.

This works great for the first few years until a ticking noise begins to develop in the engine. It is especially noticeable when you accelerate while climbing hills. A dreadful feeling of impending doom comes over you. It has to be something serious, you think.

You were on your way to the doctor's office to find out why you were so short of breath after climbing the stairs when the noise in the engine developed without warning. Not being sure what it is, you take your baby to a mechanic you trust. He examines the car and promptly tells you that the noise has started as a result of chronic use of poor quality fuel.

You sheepishly admit to him that you regularly buy the cheapest gas you can find. Being the kind of cut-rate mechanic you like, he gives you the kind of advice you came looking for. He tells you that cheap gas is okay, but that your engine will make noise and wear out sooner than it should because of the way it makes your engine dirty inside. Your car may wear out in five years instead of ten at this pace. It has been gradually building up residue, which creates more wear and tear on internal parts.

Your mechanic gives you a choice, "Start buying higher quality (and more expensive) gas, or use a fuel additive." He continues, "You can overcome some of this damage by adding one bottle of my special fuel additive at every fill up." You quickly do the math and deduce that it will still be cheaper to do this than to buy a higher grade of gas. You like your mechanic because he basically agreed with you and did not try to change your habit of buying cheap gas. This way you can continue to fill up your tank at your favorite gas station before you eat your favorite fast food. It's almost too good to be true. You tell everyone what a good mechanic and a miracle worker he is and go happily on your way!

That same day your doctor tests your blood and tells you that your cholesterol is 280 and your triglycerides are at 450. He could actually see the fat floating on your blood in the test tube. It's no wonder you are breathing hard after ascending just one flight of stairs! Your blood cannot deliver the needed oxygen to your cells because it's too full of fat!

Fortunately, you have carefully chosen your doctor by

the same criteria used to choose your mechanic. He is also the kind you like. He gives you easy choices. "Try to cut back on red meat and exercise for 30 minutes three days a week. Do this for a month and we will recheck your blood." This is all you needed to hear. Time to take action! You are only 40 years old, but a quick look in the mirror tells you that you look 60.

Starting tomorrow you order fish or chicken and fries on your regular stop for food. And, on Monday, Wednesday, and Friday you stop at the park on the way home to walk for 30 minutes. That should do it! This change was not even that hard, you think.

One month later your cholesterol is at 278 and your Triglycerides are 490. What? How could this be? With all the sacrifices you have made, how could things have gotten worse?

Thankfully, you have the best doctor in the world. He promptly tells you that you are just one of those people who are genetically predisposed to high blood lipids. "It's not your fault," he says. "And, the good news is that all you have to do is to take a pill each day and your blood fats will come down like magic. Of course, you should still watch your diet," the sympathetic doctor says. "But that is not quite as important as long as you take your pill each day. It's one of a class of "miracle drugs" called statins." If your doctor says they are miracle pills, who are you to argue? Though, something in the back of your mind doesn't completely buy into this "miracle drug" thing. You remember what your dad used to say, "If it sounds too good to be true, it probably is."

"Is it safe?" you ask. "Well sure. Millions of people take these pills," the kindly doctor retorts. "Besides, would I give you something that I don't have 100% confidence in? I take it myself," he reassures you. "Studies have confirmed its value." That's all you needed to hear.

Taking the pill each day is not the hard part for you. The cost of the prescription is! How could such a little pill that costs about 2 cents each to make, possibly cost $100 per month? Thank God you have insurance. Whew!

For six years you dutifully take your pill just as the doctor ordered. At every fill up you add one bottle of fuel treatment in your tank just like the mechanic recommended. Of course, there were a couple of days here or there when you forget (saving a few cents), but for the most part you follow instructions. It really didn't seem to make that much difference on the days you forgot. All is well. Life is good!

Then, one day you are driving along, going about your life blissfully unaware that disaster awaits you. Without a moment's notice you hear a terrible noise from under the hood and the engine ceases to run. The engine is in full arrest. It could not have come at a worse time as the extended warranty has just recently expired. Why didn't you take better care of the engine when you had the chance? Now it's too late!

It appears your miracle working mechanic's advice was not so sound in the end. You have no recourse because he is now retired and living in the Bahamas. No doubt his wealth came from selling that engine additive to everyone! Your new mechanic tells you there is no benefit in harboring any bitterness. Your old mechanic was just following the accepted protocols of the time. Now, however, your new mechanic knows better. Research has demonstrated a new and improved fuel additive that you must use in your next new car. They proved it works in closely controlled experiments involving mopeds.

To make matters worse, you have just lost your job, you have no health insurance, and you have not been feeling very well lately. Oh, woe is you. Now what? Being out of work and without insurance, you surely cannot afford to pay for the prescription bill yourself each month! It's not just the cost of the statins now. In the last year or so you have also had to start taking medicine for high blood pressure. Recently, your doctor told you he is concerned about your blood sugar. You may be diabetic! More pills, more costs.

There is no way you can afford all of these medical bills, you reason. You might just have to stop taking the pills. But then there's the pain in your muscles. And, it feels like your bones ache. You don't have any energy. It feels like you would like to sleep all day, yet you don't sleep well at night. What is going on? No matter what, you can't afford to buy another prescription of cholesterol pills.

Unfortunately, your doctor did not tell you about the study on people who suddenly quit taking statin drugs. Their cholesterol quickly skyrocketed to levels higher than it was originally. Many had massive heart attacks and died. It may have been in the fine print that came with the prescription, but who ever reads that? Besides, you trust your doctor.

So you choose to quit taking those drugs. This is a very risky move, but you are oblivious to the danger. Had you known this situation could occur, you may never have started taking the pills to begin with. Hindsight is 20/20. Even if you do now know the danger of stopping, how can you do it safely?

It's almost as if the drug companies lock you into taking the stuff forever. Indeed, your doctor might tell you that you need to continue taking these types of drugs for the rest of your life! Is this really the kind of health we want for our loved ones and ourselves? I think not!

Shortcuts never work as well as we think they will. Even when they do seem to work in the short term, there is always a drawback. Cars can be replaced. Health sometimes cannot be restored! If you choose to take chances with your car, go right ahead. It's only money. But please think twice about your health choices. Following conventional wisdom on health matters may come back to haunt you for the rest of your life, which will likely be substantially shortened.

Medical treatment most often represents a shortcut of some sort. Nature does not allow cheating. Medical treatment often represents an attempt to cheat at health.

The Root of the Problem

Elevated cholesterol may seem insignificant at first. After all, some people have it for years without any noticeable difficulties. You may ignore it for a while but the underlying problem grows and expands, slowly eroding your health over the years. Cholesterol becomes elevated because of the way we eat. Taking pills to lower it artificially is like using a fuel additive to cover the effects of cheap gas. Eventually, other problems, seemingly unrelated to the cholesterol problem, start to pop up. They accumulate to a point at which recognizable illness occurs. From that point on our health slowly decays, unless we work hard to change course.

Modern medicine gives relatively few choices to patients with high cholesterol. Patients with elevated total cholesterol are typically given the choice to try an inherently ineffective diet first. If that does not work, and it rarely does, they are told that they must take drugs (statins). Unfortunately these drugs are not a cure for high cholesterol. They do not correct the underlying problem that causes cholesterol to be high, incorrect diet.

The choices doctors give for *controlling* your high cholesterol are…

    A. Use diet and exercise to lower your cholesterol (which rarely works).

    B. Take statin drugs to artificially control your cholesterol.

    C. Live with the problem. (This produces a shortened and illness-plagued life, no-doubt)

Taking statin drugs locks you in as a lifelong patient. Once a statin prescription is begun, you must take them regularly without fail. That is, unless, you are one of the growing numbers of unfortunate patients who find that they cannot continue on these drugs due to the cost or side effects. In this case, you are simply out of luck! That is, if you believe this is your only avenue.

You may feel this is the right choice for you. However, the decision to take these drugs should not be taken lightly! The possibility of long term damage to muscle tissues from the use of statins was once thought to be minimal. It has recently been recognized as potentially significant.

In speaking of the damage to your muscles resulting from statin use, Dr. Bruce Cohen, chief of pediatric neurology at the Cleveland Clinic, said, "The mitochondria damage is what causes the weakness and discomfort - which isn't always reversible." (U.S. News & World Report, October 7, 2002) For these reasons, frequent follow-up blood tests are recommended for patients taking statins as a means of monitoring possible ill effects. These tests are reportedly not 100% accurate either. There likely are many things the experts do not yet know about these miracle drugs. Therefore, it is critical that patients also keep a close eye on *any* abnormal symptoms that may occur while taking statin medications.

Diet First

When your doctor discovers that your cholesterol is elevated, he will first, in all likelihood, recommend using diet to reduce it. In accordance to the PDR (Physicians Desk Reference), even the pharmaceutical companies who sell statin drugs suggest that diet be attempted first in any effort to lower cholesterol. Yet, much of the literature concedes that failure is the norm when relying solely on diet to lower cholesterol. *(Could this "helpful notice" be a*

ploy to undermine your faith in the effectiveness of diet?)
The result most certainly is an increased chance of failure.
Dietary changes recommended by groups such as the
American Heart Association are terribly inadequate to be
effective in significantly lowering cholesterol. To be sure,
the American Heart Association diet permits the
consumption of too many saturated fats to be effective in
significantly reducing cholesterol.

There is no question that dietary changes recommended
by physicians fall short of what is needed to make
productive changes in blood cholesterol levels. Several
problems exist here:

- Physicians have little or no training in nutrition.
- Proper guidelines that will *insure* success of the dietary
  approach do not exist.
- There is no incentive for doctors to emphasize the need
  for correct diet to patients. (They generally do not get
  paid well for dietary counseling.) In addition, much of
  the information physicians use to develop attitudes
  toward various treatments comes either directly or
  indirectly from the pharmaceutical companies. They
  have the least to gain from successful dietary

intervention.

- Doctors themselves are often poor examples for patients to follow with regard to health and diet. (No offense, as they are victims of their education.)

Your doctor will probably make broad generalized suggestions like decreasing fat and cholesterol intake, which are both valid points. They might suggest that you should eat less red meat, exercise more, and eat more fruits and vegetables. They might as well tell you that everything will be alright if you just add oatmeal to your diet. Like the claims about oatmeal, the doctor's dietary advice is slightly misleading. The end result is nearly always less than satisfactory because cholesterol levels fail to drop *significantly*. These recommendations would have a greater effect if they were more specific and realistic.

The result you get is not largely dependent on your genetics or metabolism or any other obscure factor. Your doctor may use these beliefs as an excuse to explain why diet failed for you. But the fact is *diet will work to lower your cholesterol and triglycerides to the degree to which it is applied*. The more you restrict the negative factors in your diet, while also increasing the positive, the more profound and rapid will be the improvement in your blood lipid profile!

Time is also an important factor here. Immediate improvement in blood profiles is not always obvious. Some changes doctors might view as being bad may occur early in efforts to improve health. For instance, I have tested my blood for various components during an extended fast. Cholesterol and uric acid, to name just two components, actually went up despite the fact that my body was making vast improvements in function. In short, it was using the blood, as often happens during a fast, as a vehicle to cast these substances out of the body. Within a short week or so after breaking the fast on fruits and vegetables, these factors came quickly into the low normal range. This occurrence, I believe, often clouds a physician's recognition of the value or harm of various dietary interventions in unhealthy subjects.

Doctor's Self-Image

It would be easier to influence change in patients' diets

if the doctor looked like a living example of incredible health, a rare occurrence. I know that I am much more likely to discuss diet with my patients when I have been carefully applying it to my own life. Otherwise, I feel too self-conscious to talk about it and lack enthusiasm.

Patients have often told me that a doctor advised them to lose weight in an effort to become healthier. Yet, the doctor himself was obese. This may be a significant reason many doctors choose not to discuss nutrition with their patients.

I do not believe anyone must be a *perfect* example of what one believes in. It is not humanly possible to be perfect, I will be the first to admit. But total belief in your recommendation is a necessity. Patients are very perceptive. Unless the physician truly believes with every fiber of his being that what he is recommending is the best for that patient, full compliance will never be reached. This pitfall is probably far more common than any of us realizes.

A Boon for Drug Makers

Statin drugs, the current holy grail of cholesterol

control, promise huge long-term profits for the drug makers. *(We are talking billions of dollars here!)* Once you begin to take these "miracle drugs", as some doctors view them, you must continue to take them forever. This makes for a nice stable financial future for the manufacturers, pharmacists, doctors, salesmen, etc, etc. But are statins really the answer to high cholesterol and resultant heart disease? This is one of the issues I hope to clarify in this book.

The argument for widespread statin use is supported by the difficulty in controlling cholesterol with diet alone. Believing that diet is the root cause of high cholesterol, I set out to discover just how hard it is to control my cholesterol. What I discovered was nothing short of incredible! I found that a whole multibillion-dollar industry has been built around several half-truths. When you finish with this book, you will see just how simple cholesterol control, as well as total health, can be. You will also fully understand the real relationship between blood cholesterol levels, your daily health, and, equally important, how you feel on a daily basis. The answer is clear and "rock solid". It is fully supported by readily available research.

You may have read some of the mainstream information

in other cholesterol books or government publications. One point is important to reiterate. It is incontrovertible. *Cholesterol control is important.* From that point on, however, you will find my views quite different from many "medical authorities".

Since I mentioned other cholesterol books, here is a good chance to plant a seed of caution in your mind. I have read many books about cholesterol. Some are a simple rehash of available medical jargon. No real harm here, just a little misleading at times, and far too complicated. When the material is too difficult to easily understand, those who really need it are turned off. The "medical authorities" also have a way of dismissing ideas that have not been produced by their own experts. It is as if health is too complex for other thinking human beings to understand, let alone make some interesting observations about it.

Others, whose authors shall remain nameless, do not agree that controlling cholesterol is important. They may try to sell you unneeded vitamin or mineral supplements, blaming heart attacks on some missing substance in your body such as calcium or magnesium. To fall into this trap, believing that cholesterol does not matter, is extremely unwise.

You can take all the supplements in the world while ignoring the hard truth. This path, however, does not lead to real health. By the end of this book you will know without a doubt just how significant cholesterol can be in your overall health and life. Then, like me, you can laugh at those TV and radio pill pushers. You will also recognize the ridiculousness of taking mega doses of vitamins and minerals for anything.

Chapter III

Medical Monopoly over Cholesterol

Since the discovery of its importance, the medical profession has claimed control of monitoring and treating your high cholesterol. Why not? They have controlled the world's health policies for over a century. The power of modern medical science can be overwhelming.

To the average person, it is miraculous, striking the average observer with a combination of fear and admiration. However, if you find yourself in awe of the power of science in performing health miracles, I offer a word of caution. With power often comes abuse. Modern medicine has become so enamored by its own power, that those who direct it have forgotten their purpose.

Is the purpose of the guardians of our health to contribute to the economy by selling expensive remedies for preventable illness? Is it to provide a comfortable living to health workers? *Or, is their purpose to maintain a stranglehold on power so that they can continue to dictate health policy to the world? So it appears.*

I may be a bit idealistic, but I see the purpose of health

leadership to promote optimum health, regardless of profit or loss. As keepers of our health, that is the charge they are obligated to accept. Modern times and the society in which we exist, however, has displaced moral purpose with scales of economy. Our health leadership has failed us miserably thus far. But it is never too late!

Daily news reports espouse the great powers that high-tech medicine has in the *"gallant fight to make us healthy"*. We see miraculous stories of lifesaving procedures and drugs. Magazine and newspaper articles are saturated with *"proof"* of modern medicine's greatness. How can we not bow down and pay homage to this wonder of the modern world? Daily news of incredible new high-tech procedures reminds me of a dictator who constantly saturates the news with inflated stories of his greatness. It represents a misguided attempt to retain power through awe and fear.

Do Not Be So Blind

We should never follow so blindly as to become complacent, mindless, or totally dependent. Remember that only a couple of centuries ago, back to time immemorial, priests and other religious men controlled health policy. Science has become the new religion of health care. There is nothing more powerful than the perception of dependence on another for health. Our society has truly arrived at this sad point in our evolution. This should never be the case, especially with regard to health. *Each of us controls all aspects of our own health.* It is the contrived perception of scientific superiority that keeps us dependent!

Unfortunately we now depend upon the federal government to "lead us" in health policy. The government blindly supports the medical monopoly on this issue. One look at our leaders should tell you that their health policies do not work. Those who have been brainwashed by the mainstream medical system dictate all government health policies. Except for the powerless Office of Alternative Health, all government health offices appear to exist solely to maintain the wealth and power of the medical economic machine. Medical doctors, traditional thinking scientists, and politicians seem to hold all appointments to offices of any importance in setting national health policy. Why this narrow view of health is permitted to continue, I do not understand. Traditional health leadership has led America into a healthcare death spiral.

What do I mean by this? Let's consider some cold, hard facts facing modern health care:

1. Many senior citizens cannot afford medications that have been prescribed to them. Some of these medications have been reported to cost many times what they cost in other countries. The office of Medicare has stooped as low as to use a lottery to determine who should receive drug discounts.

2. Health insurance has become so costly that employers can no longer afford to provide this vital assistance to their employees. Certainly no blue-collar employee can afford to buy health insurance for themselves and their families!

3. Insurance companies cannot afford to reduce premiums on health insurance because of ever-escalating drug and medical treatment costs, coupled with an increasing number of the sick and infirm.

Cozy Relationship

Because the United States government is so tight with the pharmaceutical companies, regulations that would reduce drug costs and thereby reduce their profits have been stymied. Most politicians are totally out of touch with the gravity of this situation. As elected officials, they have the best coverage money can buy. They have no idea how financially crippling health care costs are to so many taxpaying Americans. Or, they are ignoring it.

I am truly embarrassed for those elected officials who would choose to snuggle up to giant health care monopolies while turning their backs on a struggling public. These days it seems that no attempt is even made to hide the questionable dealings in government. It is as if most officials are making sure "they get theirs" before it's too late.

Take heart, though! The current healthcare system, whereby crisis care holds the main emphasis, is nearing the end of its functional lifespan. The day is nearing when this system will collapse under its own weight. There is an answer, and thankfully, it does not depend upon government leadership.

Lucky for us, however, it is within our control. You and I can make the whole system change as quickly as we choose. Although many will go through a painful adjustment process, better health for all will be the ultimate outcome. You can be ahead of the curve on this one. It is up to you.

Bitter?

You may think I sound bitter toward modern medicine, but I am not. I have tremendous respect for medical doctors. They are bright, well educated, and serve daily to save many lives from the brink of death. Their capabilities are inspiring, although these accomplishments pale in comparison to that of the natural healing ability of all creatures living under optimum conditions.

I admire doctors' abilities and resources. At the same time, I am dumbfounded by their lack of meaningful leadership. They have held control of public health policy for generations, yet wholly preventable chronic disease continues to escalate. We live longer as a whole, but the quality of life for the majority of the elderly has much to be desired. Old age has become a costly and burdensome chore. For many, even middle age is a painful experience.

In the truest sense, high-tech medicine's miraculous cures are little more than proverbial fingers in the dike, which holds back an ever-growing flood of illness. The pills they prescribe can do little to correct illness. Though they may make you feel "well" temporarily, medicine has nothing to do with wellness. It has only to do with disease. **But for greed and power, we might all enjoy perfect health!**

The answer to our suffering and infirmity is known. Researchers have discovered why we suffer to such a large degree throughout our artificially shortened natural life. The brightest of them know why we die far short of potential 120-150 year lifespan. Yet, our profit driven health care system has failed miserably in using this information to lead Americans to a much healthier, happier life. Health information is distributed to the public to the degree at which it can produce a profit. No matter how relevant the information is to our health, if it cannot be translated into profit, it is not promoted.

While the research community shamelessly begs for more money to fund the next "promising study", we continue to suffer and die in droves. "We are close to an answer," drones the familiar voice of the researcher's public relations machine. "One more million, or ten, or maybe 100 million dollars is all we need." "The answer is right around the corner," they say. Yet, the answer never really seems to come, does it? All we get are more questions that need to be answered.

Let's be honest here. We are all responsible for letting this situation fester. We have sacrificed millions of lives of our loved ones by placing all of our hope into one basket, high-tech research. Our refusal to take responsibility for our own actions has allowed painful disease and disability to become woven into the very fabric of our society.

We cannot however, accept full responsibility for this situation. Health care leaders have the power and the knowledge to change our health for the better. But, an entrenched system of drug sales in the billions of dollars, expensive surgeries, and resultant lifelong patients has kept the current system of crisis care intact. Except for greed and power, we might all enjoy perfect health! So excuse me if I am just a little bitter.

I am deeply saddened by the lives lost in the trade towers on 9-11-2001, but there is something that does not seem logical to me. For the loss of those 3,000 lives we declare war on terrorism, spending billions of dollars and risking many, many lives. I applaud this decision. Yet, at the same time in America, millions of innocents have been killed by negligent health policies, and we accept this as normal daily life?

If I am bitter, there is good reason. Am I the only one who sees the immorality of this whole picture? There is so much more to life than limping from one illness to another. We are but sheep. We feed the "economy god" with our health sacrifices. You and I are being duped into forfeiting a gift that has truly been given to us by God Almighty, the gift of wonderful health. Ironically, those who profit from our misdirection are fooled by their own exuberance for a weak and near sighted health philosophy. The wealth resulting from our eager acceptance of their methods has caused them to believe in this system's superiority. They are truly blinded by success to the point of buying into the system themselves.

To change this we must look past glitzy advertising and

short-term illusions of good health to find real health. There is never a need for sickness when the rules of health are followed. It is my opinion that modern medicine is remiss in its duty to provide us all with the best health possible. Yet, they are probably guilty only of not seeing the forest for the trees.

Misplaced Focus

The misplaced focus on crisis type care is not a malicious act by physicians or other health care workers. It is the result of an elaborate system that has evolved over the decades. It is a system that rewards practices within the status quo. Freethinking and genuine innovation is punished. It provides no incentives to the doctor or the patient for prevention through the most effective avenues, "real nutrition" and exercise. This faulty system gives the appearance of providing the best care available anywhere in the world, yet consistently ranks behind many less technologically advanced countries in overall health. (World Health Organization)

Laws and public health policies that will not permit change support this system. The government is concerned about the economy. The drug lobby, physicians groups, cattlemen, dairy industry middlemen, hospital and nursing home lobbies are each busy looking out for number one. Seldom is their best interest in our best interest. Truly, there is no lobby for real health!

Lobbying by these influential and wealthy professional groups to maintain their economic advantage is considered acceptable behavior. It sickens me to think that money matters more to them than our health. It has become a commodity to be bought and sold at the highest price.

Caring for sick people accounts for over 20% of our national economy. If everyone suddenly became healthy, our economy would likely collapse. A sizable chunk of our nation's economy is built upon the backs of the sick. More importantly, our future economy is tied to your future contribution. *You are cordially invited to follow in the sickly footsteps of those who went before you.* To avoid the fate of all your loved ones who went before you to a painful and untimely death, you must open your mind to change.

Therein lies my only criticism of modern medicine. I concede that if it were not for the great care of well-trained physicians and nurses, I would probably not have lived to this point. Few others can say different. But I also know that the truth about health has been recognized for over a century. Some mostly unknown, very intelligent and honest doctors from various professions tried to spread the truth with great resistance. Had this knowledge not been suppressed for all that time, I might have enjoyed perfect health all through my early years, hardly needing medical care but for cases of accident.

Truth Be Known

Fortunately I have now discovered the joys of total health independence that were missing for the past 43 years. I fully intend to relish it and to share it with others to the best of my ability despite the substantial risks involved. When the day comes that I am prevented from speaking the truth about health, you, having read this book, are responsible for passing it on to others.

Crisis care has a place in the future of American health care. It will, however, be a much smaller part than it currently enjoys. It will be focused on that area in which doctors truly excel, emergency medicine. The care provided to accident victims is a shining example of the best medicine has to offer.

I cannot help but believe that many, many medical doctors are incredibly frustrated in their daily practice. No matter how financially successful, they are extremely ineffectual in producing long-term health improvements in their patients. Being an intelligent bunch, it must be painfully obvious to many that their methods only produce temporary results. It must be an incredible burden to bear. Perhaps this accounts, in part, for the high rate of physician drug abuse and suicide. I invite all physicians to jump into preventative health care with both feet!

Personal Experience

I would like to end this chapter with a little story: My mother was in the hospital after feeling light headed and suffering some chest discomfort. She was put into a room on the heart floor where she could be monitored and tested.

I was visiting with her one day, when the cardiologist appeared with the results of her tests. He was pleasant and more supportive than anyone could have asked. He explained that she had unstable angina. She had at least 3 coronary arteries that were significantly blocked from years of traditional diet.

The cardiologist explained the treatment options. He also warned her of the dangers of non-treatment. The picture was not rosy. To make a long story short, she had stents placed into her coronary arteries and, at this writing, is doing well.

One thing that truly astounded me, however, was the meal that was provided to her while I was there. Everyone knows that as a general rule, we should decrease the amount of saturated fats in our diet. This advice is especially important for heart patients, as you will see in the chapter discussing blood viscosity. Her meal was indeed marked as a "heart smart" meal. When I opened the lid, imagine my surprise to find a pork chop, gravy, mashed potatoes, green beans, butter (or margarine) pats, and a white dinner roll!

I took the written menu home with me. Upon analyzing it on a computer program, I found that it contained a whopping 43% fat. Total fat consumption for the *average person* is recommended to be below 30%, even by conservative standards. Why would they give a heart patient a meal that is over 40% fat?

The significance of this will become obvious later in this book. For patients with symptomatic blockage of coronary arteries, one high fat meal can be deadly. For now, suffice it to say that this speaks volumes about medical understanding and application of diet. It probably says more about hospital oversight of meal planning. In medical settings, the significance of diet takes a back seat to profitable and immediate life saving procedures.

Interestingly, I quizzed my mother's cardiologist about the value of diet in altering blood viscosity (thickness) in cases of angina. I explained to him that studies had shown that using a process called apheresis (artificially filtering fats from the blood), angina could be eliminated, negating the need for invasive and dangerous surgery. These studies, done primarily in Europe, are numerous and conclusive. They pointed to the fact that eating a very low fat diet could also reduce blood viscosity, albeit more gradually than apheresis does. He was unaware of these studies.

This illustrates something I think limits progress in

American health care. Physicians who specialize in one area of medicine often become more like technicians than doctors. They are very good at certain procedures they perform regularly. However, they may become so dogmatic in their approach that they fail to keep an open eye for newer procedures. This is especially true if the new procedures are less popular and less profitable.

It is important to recognize the power of diet in correcting aberrant bodily functions that permit disease. Diet truly has the ability to make us well. The real beauty of God's gift appears to those who apply it consistently.

Here, supreme health is absolute.

Chapter IV

The Drug "Cure" for Cholesterol

So you gave it a good 2 or 3 months eating less red meat, butter, and cheese, and eating more oatmeal, fish, and chicken. You made such *great sacrifices*, but to no avail. Your cholesterol only came down a relatively few points. It must be your metabolism. Perhaps you are genetically prone to high cholesterol. "It's not your fault," your doctor might say. You are just one of the many unlucky patients who cannot reduce their cholesterol with diet and exercise. "We'll get you started on a statin prescription," he or she might say in a kindly voice. "I know that will bring it down."

There is no question; your doctor believes he is doing what is best for you. As a matter of fact, using statins as a crutch to reduce your cholesterol while correcting your diet to become truly healthy "may not" be such a bad idea. Of course, extreme caution should be exercised here. The nature of any drug mandates that it have side effects. It has been said in the past that a drug without side effects is no drug at all. Statins definitely fit the definition of a drug.

Big Decisions

The commitment to begin taking statin drugs should not be taken lightly. Along with the general risk of developing health problems while taking these or any drugs, there are other potentially deadly side effects associated with stopping statin therapy. An important study was authored by Heeschen, Hamm, Laufs, Snapinn, Bohm, and White of Germany and published in the journal *Circulation* in 2002. This study and others like it appear to demonstrate a link between the withdrawal of statin treatment during acute heart symptoms and an increased risk of further episodes or death. The increased risk was greater than the risk for heart patients who never received statin therapy. Furthermore, patients admitted to the hospital who quit taking their statins were reportedly 3 times as likely to have heart attacks as those who continued to take them. This is an interesting study for several reasons.

- First, it should make you think long and hard before choosing to go on a prescription for statins. You should be very sure that you are able to continue them for the rest of your life. What if your insurance runs out? Can you afford $70 to $100 per month for a prescription? Will you remain committed to this therapy for a lifetime?

- Second, you should be wondering when this threefold risk for heart attack begins. Are you at increased risk immediately after missing just one dose even in the absence of symptoms? What if you forget a dose or two? What if you were several hours late in taking a dose one day? I have not seen studies that answer these questions.

- Lastly, how long does the increased risk last after withdrawing statin drug therapy? Will you return to normal risk levels after you are off them for a month, a year?

There is no way to know exactly how many of the thousands of heart attacks that occur in the United States each day are related to someone who simply decided to stop taking their medication. Then again, this provides an easy excuse for those times when the statins do not prevent a heart attack even when taken as directed. There are no statistics, to my knowledge, which statistically account for the number of cardiac and cardiovascular events suffered by those who take statins as directed.

Remember that for many years it was *"assumed"* that hormone replacement therapy was supposed to reduce the chance of heart attack. That has since been proven wrong. Why did it take so long to figure that out? The same lack of vital statistics may exist with statins today.

This information concerns me very much. I fear for the patients out there who suddenly find themselves without insurance coverage and lack the significant financial fortitude to pay for their own prescriptions. You can bet, however, that the drug companies are working on some form of legislation to help everyone get "free" statins via federal insurance coverage. This would mean we all pay for them, whether we take them or not.

If statins really were a miracle drug as the claims go, there would be a strong argument for mass distribution. Of course, as we have seen throughout history, it does not always take much to get a bill passed when you own the legislative process, as large drug corporations and the medical establishment do. (*One need only look at recently passed (2004) Medicare legislation to believe this.*) Merit is not always a requirement.

On the other hand, I fear for the patients now taking

statins who want to correct their diet, lower their cholesterol naturally, and eventually get off cholesterol medications all together. Will they take this study to mean that they can never go without statins? I also wonder if misinformed doctors will believe this leaves their patients no option in this situation.

In chess this is called checkmate. The patient is damned if he does and damned if he doesn't. I cannot help but envision the fat cat pharmaceutical CEO's smiling ear to ear at this thought. Business loves to have consumers desire their products. A product that consumers believe they cannot live without is a perpetual grand slam.

How Statins Prevent Heart Attacks

The previously mentioned study certainly can be alarming. However, there is a very basic and understandable reason people with high cholesterol have heart attacks. In my opinion, it is also the reason quitting statins increases the risk of heart attack so greatly and so quickly. You will see that quitting statins can be healthful rather than dangerous when done properly. (It should only be done under your doctor's supervision.) Do not fear! We'll keep this simple and understandable.

According to accepted scientific theory, statins work specifically to reduce the cholesterol levels in your blood. It does this by two mechanisms. First, it reduces cholesterol production by the liver. Second, it causes the liver to remove cholesterol from the blood at a higher rate than normal. Additionally, it appears to reduce triglyceride levels in the blood.

* Numerous studies point out that when your cholesterol and/or triglyceride levels are too high; you are more prone to developing arteriosclerosis, (narrowing of arteries due to plaquing). This is thought to be the major cause of heart attacks and strokes. When the arteries get too narrow, blood can no longer flow through them efficiently. This happens suddenly when a clot forms (as they often do in the body) and gets stuck where the artery narrows. The heart cells (in heart attacks) or the brain cells (in strokes) quickly suffer and die from a lack of oxygen and other nutrients. This basic relationship is very well documented.

Why Do Plaques Form?

What is not well understood, however, is how and why this plaquing occurs. Scientists often speak of the process of oxidation whereby the artery walls are damaged by the body's response to excessive amounts of cholesterol or harmful chemicals in the blood. This causes the cholesterol to grab onto the roughened arterial walls, thereby developing a foothold for the development of plaques. Thus arteries gradually grow narrow.

No matter the specific origins of the process, there is some convincing evidence supporting the importance of cholesterol in this whole scenario. According to the Merck Manual, studies on monkeys have demonstrated that plaque begins to build up inside artery walls *within just two weeks* of the onset of hypercholesterolemia (increased cholesterol in the blood). The elevated levels of cholesterol in the monkey's blood were caused by a cholesterol and saturated fat rich diet. Now, if someone tries to tell you that cholesterol really does not matter, you know better!

There are various arguments describing differing views of the cause of cholesterol adhering to the artery wall. No one really knows for sure what the specific cause is. It should be noted that the type of diet that increases cholesterol also contributes of other negative products accumulating in the blood. One of these is homocysteine. It is thought to be an irritant to the artery walls. Indeed, homocysteine levels are directly proportional to an increase incidence of heart attack. Elevated homocysteine is very common in those who eat a western diet.

One other interesting and I think crucial piece to this puzzle has to do with the effect fats have on the blood itself. Cholesterol and triglycerides are substances that increase blood viscosity. That is, they make your blood thicker. The more cholesterol and triglycerides in your blood, the thicker it becomes. Thicker blood is more difficult for the heart to pump around the body than thinner blood. This naturally slows down the flow. Add to this the narrowing most people over the age of 30 have in their arteries, and it is easy to see how blood flow is slowed to a stop at times.

Parallels in Nature

We can see this process readily in other examples in nature. When streams flow freely and rapidly, little, if any, buildup of sediment and debris is seen. Yet, slow the stream down by adding large amounts of suspended matter such as mud, branches, and rocks, and the result is obvious. Slow buildup of sediment, rocks, and trees gradually brings the stream to a halt. The result is a backup of water and often increased pressure. In the human body, of course, this whole process is complicated by obscure and complicated physiological changes. But, the process is basically similar in many ways.

When this process occurs in our body, the cholesterol has more time to grab onto the inside of your arteries. Chemical reactions take place, which might not otherwise be given the opportunity. This accounts for the gradual narrowing of blood vessels. Chemical irritation of artery walls result in the production of scar tissue as a means of repair material. When enough of this fibrous tissue clumps together, it can break loose, creating a clot in the blood. This can quickly result in a heart attack or stroke.

Benefits of Statins

The real benefit of statins is in the reduction of cholesterol, essentially a solid non-dissolved particle in the blood. Removing excess cholesterol from the blood is the equivalent of getting the sticks out of a slow moving stream. Removing cholesterol from the blood reduces blood viscosity (thickness) by taking out the "sticks". This makes the blood thinner and easier for the heart to pump.

If not for all the potential side effects, both known and unknown, statins would be a great, albeit partial, answer to the problem of heart attacks and strokes.

With this in mind, we can now more clearly understand how the withdrawal of statins can be achieved without risk. The use of statins and the use of diet can be viewed as somewhat parallel paths to reducing cholesterol. One path, statins, reduces cholesterol to an arbitrary level in the blood. It also carries with it significant risk for some, in my opinion, and it is very expensive. The other path, proper diet, has no bad physical side effects, can reduce cholesterol fully to the body's perfect levels, and saves huge amounts of money in the form of grocery costs and health bills for future sickness.

Both of these methods are successful in preventing heart attacks, strokes, Alzheimer's, and very likely many other disease processes. Their success in these areas is due to the reduction of cholesterol and triglycerides resulting in reduced blood viscosity (thickness). *In chapter 8, I will explain why blood viscosity influences health more than any other conceivable factor.*

So it is understandable that the reason for increased risk of heart attack after withdrawing statins is related to a sudden increase in cholesterol and triglycerides. The resulting rapid elevation of blood viscosity places tremendous stress on the heart. Suddenly the heart must once again pump sludge around the body instead of significantly thinner blood. With the increased workload on the heart comes an increased need for oxygen and other vital nutrients by the heart cells. The harder the heart muscle works, the more oxygen it needs. Thicker blood makes delivery of oxygen and energy to these cells impossible.

Let us add in the presumption that the coronary arteries, which supply this heart with blood, are partially clogged. Combine with that, the blood passing through those arteries has suddenly become thicker and sticky. This is a devastating cascade of events for this poor heart. Now can you see why the withdrawal of statins can triple the risk of a heart attack?

A Positive Note

It should be noted here that statin use has been associated with decreased risk of Alzheimer's disease and, quite possibly, osteoporosis. This is not marketing hype by the drug companies. I believe statins will ultimately be found helpful with other diseases like arthritis and Parkinson's as well. This will be detailed further in chapter 8, which deals with the extensive effects of blood viscosity on overall human health. Rest assured that any claim made for the benefits of taking statins goes double for diet.

This connection between statin use and various other disease processes solidifies my claim that blood viscosity is at the very root of health or illness. Proper diet will provide all of these benefits without risk. The choice to become healthy is yours alone and requires only a conscious decision and a concerted effort.

Possible Side Effects of Statin Drugs

As a means of helping you to avoid permanent health problems, some documented side effects of statins will be offered here. If you are taking any of the cholesterol lowering drugs and suffer any of these symptoms, you should discuss it with your doctor. Patients taking statins during clinical trials reported the following side effects. They are not specific for any one brand. This should not be considered a complete list.

Note Non-medical terms have been used where possible.

{Gas, constipation, indigestion and/or stomach ache, chest pain, vague feeling of depression or illness, nausea, vomiting, ulceration of the mouth or stomach, difficulty swallowing, inflammation of the liver or pancreas, yellowish coloration of the skin, shortness of breath, difficulty sleeping, dizziness, prolonged drowsiness, arthritis, leg cramps, muscle pain, itchy skin.}

By far, the most significant side effect that has been associated with statin drugs is rhabdomyolysis (breakdown of muscle). It is indicated by muscle pain and progressive weakness.

This was the primary reason for the recall of one of the most popular statins. It has also ignited an increasing awareness of the possibility that a much larger, hidden danger could exist with statin use. As with most drugs, which appear harmless in the early stages of use, the ugly side may not reveal itself for years to come with long-term use.

American Heart Association President, David Faxon, M.D. has said, "Patients on any statin who have experienced side effects such as muscle aches or dark urine should stop taking the drug and immediately consult their physician." (American College of Cardiology and American Heart Association Advisory, 2001)

Personal Experience

I had firsthand experience with a patient who, while on a prescription for one of the statin drugs, described experiencing increasing weakness with a great deal of muscle pain. She finally became so weak that she lost her ability to walk. She initially thought she had arthritis or fibromyalgia. It was only through extensive rehabilitation lasting several months that she recovered. She was one of the lucky ones. Interestingly, her doctor prescribed this drug even though her total cholesterol reportedly was barely above 200. *(Remember that most doctors consider this to be normal cholesterol.)* Unbelievably, once she had recovered, the doctor suggested she try another brand of statin!

Her response was understandable, "No thanks!"

Note A class action lawsuit has been filed over the problems arising from this statin. It has been withdrawn from the market.

It is also possible that you may have symptoms or side effects not listed here. This becomes especially true when one or more other medications are combined with statins. If you suspect a problem with your medications, especially if you note the onset of new symptoms within a couple of weeks of starting a prescription, ask your doctor. Do not become complacent if you have no adverse effects in the first weeks. As with any drug, side effects can develop at any time during use.

Talk to your doctor about every little symptom you suspect may be related to the drugs you take. And remember, doctors can at times become somewhat defensive about the medications they have prescribed. Do not be afraid to press your doctor on this matter. It has been estimated that between 100,000 and 200,000 people die each year as a result of medical mistakes and prescription drug reactions. (A figure supported by U.S. government research.) A little caution could be your only defense. Your life may ultimately depend upon your persistence.

In closing, statins may indeed be the miracle they have been proclaimed to be. Maybe the vast majority of patients can take this medication without serious side effects. You could depend totally on this drug alone to reduce your cholesterol, failing to follow the suggested low fat diet as is recommended with the drug. You might live somewhat healthier despite poor dietary choices. But then, you could have all of these benefits and more, with none of the risk.

Nature has a way of making us pay for our dietary indiscretions. Historically, it seems that every "miracle drug" is eventually found to have some important, often devastating, drawbacks. You should understand by now that elevated cholesterol is truly a major part of the problem with our poor health in America. It is not, however, the whole picture. That is multifaceted. Statins deal only with a small portion of these problems. In addition, as a drug, it automatically carries with it some significant risk. If there were a better way that does not involve the risky path of drug dependence, wouldn't it be better to go this route?

Getting Off Statins

There is reason for great joy and celebration here! God has provided us a way to safely and quickly eliminate the need for statin drugs. The key to successful elimination of statins without the concomitant risk of heart attack is to utilize diet to reduce cholesterol naturally, before stopping the drug. Your blood viscosity can be normalized, by removing *the causative factor* of high cholesterol, poor food choices. Therefore, the underlying problem is solved before statins are withdrawn.

The trick here is to know when to stop taking the statins. I have seen some patients who, while taking statins, improve their diet to the point at which their blood cholesterol levels plummet. Though their doctor knows the patient is on a low fat diet and is monitoring their cholesterol levels, they hesitate to stop the medication.

Some doctors simply do not understand that diet can affect cholesterol this significantly and this quickly. Others feel that the reduction will only be temporary. Their experience is that patients are generally weak willed and likely will revert to less advantageous, normal eating habits. This is a common problem to which I will offer a tenable solution in this book.

So we might understand why doctors would be reluctant to stop drug therapy for high cholesterol. Remember too, doctors are trained to believe that once a patient begins statin therapy, they will be on it for life! This is an errant belief, which may harm millions of patients.

For most statin users who choose to reduce cholesterol by diet, there comes a time of reckoning. Strict adherence to the diet will result in dramatic decreases in blood cholesterol and triglyceride levels. *(My cholesterol dropped over 30 points per week, as did my triglycerides!)* Unfortunately, statins like all drugs are dumb. That is, the drug only has one function, lowering cholesterol. It does not "know" to lower it less or more. The result could be an excessive decrease in cholesterol levels. Your doctor should monitor blood cholesterol levels if you follow any diet to reduce it. I checked my cholesterol weekly.

Test Your Own Cholesterol

There is now a means for testing your cholesterol at home. This is a great way to help your doctor to monitor the change you will see with the improvement in diet. It also represents a neat way that you can check the effect of different foods on your cholesterol levels once you have achieved maximum improvement. *You will be surprised by the difference one burger and fries can make in your cholesterol!*

The name of one company who provides home testing products for cholesterol is **Lifestream® Technologies, Inc.** Their website is located at: **KnowItForLife.com.** They can also be reached at 1-877-416-1100.

The cost of the equipment is about $120 to get started. Beyond that it will cost you less than $5 per test. This is a substantial savings in time and money compared to having it tested at a lab or doctors' office. The accuracy of this device is very good. I highly recommend purchasing one.

I suggest you test once per week for a few months. Track the way diet influences your cholesterol levels. Keep a log of your tests. This way you can get a feel for, and get excited about how easy it is to lower cholesterol.

Changes

When you begin eating the foods that were meant for your body, changes take place. Your body begins to function normally, although it may not seem like it to you initially. The liver no longer has *extra* garbage to deal with. The *extra* saturated fat that you normally eat is not present. Therefore, your liver stops producing *extra* cholesterol. With a decrease in calorie consumption, the liver does not have to package *extra* calories as fat. So, the amount of fat in your blood (triglycerides) plummets.

But there is a temporary problem accompanying these marvelous adaptations and adjustments. If you do not understand what is happening, it may scare you and your doctor. The statins were artificially lowering cholesterol, triglycerides, and even blood pressure before proper diet was introduced. With dietary adaptation comes natural improvement of these processes. The body acts to normalize things, but the statins push cholesterol and triglyceride levels below normal. Blood pressure often drops as a result of decreased blood viscosity (thickness). The result is a constant tired feeling, possible light-headedness, headaches and weakness.

Is the diet the cause of these worrisome symptoms? Should you stop the diet? Not necessarily. You need to see your doctor immediately! Tell him you want his permission to stop taking the statins! Within days to a week, you will begin to feel tremendous. Energy levels will skyrocket. A wonderful sense of well-being will be yours.

If your doctor has concerns, respect his opinion and follow his advice. But be somewhat persistent. If you are truly following this diet, excluding significant other problems, you will see the changes I speak of here.

Caution: *Statin use should only be withdrawn under your doctor's supervision. He is the best judge of when to stop taking prescribed medications. This may take some convincing on your part and should not be attempted until you have stabilized your cholesterol by a consistent pattern of low fat eating. I encourage you to work with your doctor.*

Chapter V

Pills, Potions, Food Cures, and Other Half Truths

Since the concept of high cholesterol first evolved to a level of international consciousness, some "experts" have downplayed its importance. Recently, I saw an influential doctor on a television talk show. He said that cholesterol plaques are not the real culprits in heart attack. He noted that it was a clot that formed as a result of the body's attempt to repair damaged artery walls that were the real cause. I say this is splitting hairs. A diet that causes cholesterol build up in the blood is the root cause of all of these circulatory problems, and I will show you how.

Some authorities try to convince us that having elevated cholesterol is of no consequence to our health. They might say that the real culprit in the narrowing of or damage to the arteries is a vitamin or mineral deficiency. Their angle is that cholesterol is only an innocent bystander in the whole process of forming circulatory disease. You must realize, however, that these "experts" have a hidden agenda. **They want you to buy their supplements, no**

doubt!

These modern day snake oil salesmen often have the dubious distinction of being a "noted researcher" or some other impressive credential to draw you into believing their less than complete story. Their goal is to create just enough doubt in your mind to cause you to buy their product. Some of these doctors may have nothing to do with the development of the product they are hawking. They merely allow the use of their name and credentials in exchange for monetary reward. So much for the validity of scientific process and the value of credentials!

The sales pitch is that by taking some special form of calcium, vitamin C, an herb, or some other "miracle concoction", cholesterol will be prevented from causing narrowing of your arteries. These chemical substances supposedly will interfere with the detrimental plaquing process. Thus, the body can continue functioning normally despite the uninterrupted presence of excess cholesterol.

There are difficulties in proving or disproving these theories. One problem is that cholesterol buildup in the arteries is such a slow process as to make it impossible to know in a short period of time whether these supplements help or not. Many variables such as diet and exercise habits further complicate the results when comparing one person to the next.

Like the fabled snake oil salesmen of the past, the modern sellers of these pills and potions use this inability to disprove their approach to their own advantage. Creating doubt in the consumer's mind about the value of reducing cholesterol in the blood gives them an opportunity to sell you a product "proven to work". This works very well. Especially well if the consumer believes there is no need to make any sacrifices in their beloved lifestyle to achieve better health. You simply take these pills or powders and go on about your life as you always have. *Wouldn't it be great if that were really possible?*

Regardless of the facts, or lack thereof behind the argument, this line of thinking has caused many consumers to become skeptical about the importance of cholesterol and its influence on their health. I have met many elderly patients who have been duped by these baseless claims.

This is bad. The battle to reduce cholesterol in the blood is difficult enough by virtue of what is necessary to change it, a better diet. To be effective it actually requires a change in lifestyle. Add to this, the public's wavering on whether cholesterol reduction is necessary at all, and convincing them to change their diet and lifestyle to achieve better cholesterol becomes nearly impossible.

Half Truths

Cereal companies claim that eating their products can do the trick in reducing cholesterol. Vitamin sellers suggest that niacin can bring it down. Exercise fanatics will tell you that you simply do not exercise enough. Your doctor might suggest that diet cannot do it, so you need the help of statin drugs. With all of these cures available, what fool would go to the trouble of changing their diet? After all, no one has really proved that eating differently will actually make you healthier anyway! Have they?

Well, I have. The proof is in this book if you choose to accept it. If you were to apply it, you could prove it to yourself. I have dedicated my life to helping everyone who wishes to become and stay well, to see the truth about health. The information in this book may not be a double blind study, carried out at some fancy-pants university, but it is the honest truth. Because it is based on truth, I am willing to stand behind it to my death. Can you make that statement about anything?

Just in case my word is not good enough, however, there is at least one recent study that proves diet can match the results of statin drugs. Research directed by Cyril Kendall of the University of Toronto, Canada demonstrated that (LDL) blood cholesterol could be reduced as much as 35% in one month simply by eating a vegetarian based diet. Unfortunately, the diet they used is not what I would recommend.

The dieters in this study consumed okra, eggplant, and large amounts of a fiber-based laxative (the maker of which probably sponsored the study) every day. This would not be very appealing. As a matter of fact, it is ridiculous!

It is quite possible to reduce cholesterol levels in the blood while enjoying much more flavorful natural foods. The laxative is totally unnecessary. This study does prove, however, that a dietary approach to the problem of high cholesterol definitely does work. You will find the diet I ate to lower my cholesterol 30% in 3 weeks much more palatable.

Your Choice

What you do with the information I provide here is up to you. There is probably no way for me to convince you that what I have done here represents the most remarkable thing you can do for your health and longevity, but it is. And, there is one more thing that I know for certain. **If you continue to rely on pills and potions, which always fail to *resolve the cause* of your health problems, you will be no healthier in one year than you are right now.**

I am confident that my health is improving each and every day that I follow the rules for health! It will continue to improve until the end of my joyous and fulfilling life. You can have that same confidence in your health. The choice is yours. Choose carefully. Each year that goes by living as you now do, will surely add to your misery and decrease your overall lifespan.

Oh, I Give Up!

I know many patients who have given up on lowering

cholesterol, no matter what course of treatment they choose. Some have tried the high priced statin drugs because it seemed like the easy way. And besides, insurance paid for it. (The insurance companies have much to learn too.) Many patients gave up on these drugs when their muscles and bones started to ache. Some stayed with it until insurance changes forced them to stop.

Nearly all have tried the weak and ineffective traditional dietary changes recommended by their doctor. The vast majority of those failed too. Vitamins, minerals, and herbs are sometimes helpful in making small changes in cholesterol levels in the body. Remember that high cholesterol is the result of dietary excesses, not deficiencies. So, how could a supplement fix this problem?

Worst of all, if you do not have your cholesterol tested to see if the supplements corrected the problem, you may be walking around with a false sense of security. This happens when people take the advertiser's word as gospel, never testing the theory.

Niacin has been shown to reduce cholesterol a little, but it can cause hot flashes, a sure sign of chemical imbalance. Garlic can also help. Studies prove that a maceration of onion and garlic, taken daily, can reduce cholesterol levels slightly. But do you really want to smell like garlic and onions all the time? I have met people who use this approach. It is difficult to have an extended conversation with them due to the smell! It oozes from every pore. They are the only ones who don't recognize it.

All of these methods, from drugs to supplements and herbs, have a positive effect, however small and temporary, by artificially reducing cholesterol levels. They are no more than temporary ways of tiptoeing around the central underlying issue. You may find fleeting success with these "cures", but their value is limited over the long haul. Also, most treatment methods are extremely limited in the degree of improvement they provide. Failure to fix high cholesterol by these methods often makes people feel that there is no hope. But, I promise you there is hope beyond your wildest dreams and beyond the ridiculous claims you have heard for these cures.

I beg you to understand that no matter how many failures you have suffered in your attempts to lower cholesterol, you should not give up! Failure should not belittle the importance of attaining a healthy cholesterol level in your blood. Your failure is simply the result of having been led down the wrong path. There is proof that controlling cholesterol is a key component to improving the health of your blood and in preventing heart disease and stroke. It is also a critical step in becoming as healthy as you were designed by God to be. We must strive for optimum health. Denying this responsibility is a slap in the Face of God.

False Hopes

I would like to say a word or two here about fad diets. Confusion abounds when it comes to a healthy diet. Specifically, I would like to address the high protein, high fat, low-carbohydrate diet. This is the diet Dr. Robert C. Atkins advocated to help patients lose weight. Dr. Atkins was very successful in helping many people to lose weight, of that I have no doubt.

High fat diets like Dr. Atkins' can certainly help you to lose weight. The question that must be asked of any diet, however, is at what cost? Losing weight *can* be a benefit to your health. You will get no argument from me on this point. There are limitations to that statement, however. Just because you are losing weight does not necessarily mean you are becoming healthy. People with cancer for instance, are known to lose significant weight. Would you call them healthy? I also have met extremely unhealthy individuals who were as skinny as toothpicks. Being thin obviously was not the only health factor influencing their life.

Lately there has been a huge amount of attention given to America's obesity problem. Of course we are not the only country with a weighty problem. Most industrialized countries follow suit with the increased use of processed foods that often accompanies a mechanized lifestyle. Exercise is necessarily decreased at the same time. This certainly makes the reason for obesity obvious.

Misplaced Emphasis

It is my contention, however, that the emphasis on obesity will get us nowhere in our fight to be healthy. Granted, it has been proved that decreased calorie consumption improves health and longevity. Roy Walford, M.D. demonstrated this clearly in his book, "Beyond the

120 Year Diet." Others have done equally impressive studies back through history.

To focus only on weight without increased attention to the quality of the menu is short sighted and unproductive. What overweight person wouldn't give anything to be thin? Yet society's weight problem has changed little statistically as obesity rates continue to skyrocket.

I have often said in lectures that you can follow a diet of chocolate bars and lose weight. The response I typically get is, "Can you show me that diet?" This is very telling about our attitudes regarding diet. It is something we must come to grips with if we are ever to become truly healthy. If you ate fewer calories than you use each day, you would lose weight no matter what you eat. Certainly, losing weight, while eating the most nutritious food available, would be the healthiest method.

Fasting is the quickest way to lose weight. I have lost over a pound each day while fasting. Though there are long-term benefits from a properly managed fast, the immediate process is a breakdown of body structure. Fasting can be exceedingly healthful, done correctly, because it cleanses the body of many, many unnecessary byproducts of metabolism. It frees the body's resources and improves energy efficiency, much like a good tune-up does for your car.

Both the candy bar diet and the fast have weight loss in common. That is the only thing they have in common. The fast can produce supreme health with proper post-fast re-feeding. The candy bar diet will undoubtedly undermine health to new and unpredictable lows.

It is critical to understand that all maintenance processes in the body continue while dieting, even fasting. One really important process is that of blood cell production. The body will continue to build new cells during even the strictest diet, using whatever raw materials it has available to it at the time. If you are eating junk, the outcome will be that the new cells produced during this time will basically be junk! This point will become very clear in a later chapter.

Therefore, losing weight should not be considered the total answer to any health problem. Being overweight is not a disease. It is merely a symptom of wrong eating and living. It is not the cause of diabetes, breathing difficulties, psoriasis, or cancer. There is no question, however, that obesity is often a sign of a diet that will lead to these and many other diseases.

The Debate Continues

Articles supporting the high fat / high protein approach to weight loss, describe it as being superior to low fat diets. This may be the case when the carbohydrates are something other than fruits and vegetables. The type of carbohydrates consumed is critical to the success or failure of the diet in producing good health. Processed and refined carbohydrates such as pastas, breads, sweetened cereals, candy, cakes, juices, sodas, and low fat sweet snacks are poor choices for dietary success. Weight loss is minimal and poor health will quickly result from the poor nutrition provided by these foods. I can certainly see where a high fat diet might seem superior to these foods in some ways. Who in their right mind, though, would even consider these previously mentioned junk foods to be a good choice for anyone?

Consuming refined carbohydrates and saturated fats together raises cholesterol and triglycerides. Eliminating simple carbohydrates, while eating saturated fats, will reduce triglycerides greatly and cholesterol slightly. Weight loss is a natural outcome. Patients on the high fat diet are also likely to eat fewer calories as a result of the filling effects of fats and the relatively low calorie menu. This accounts for some weight loss. However, no diet that recommends the elimination of fruit from the diet can be considered healthy!

Significant complaints about the low carbohydrate diet, by those who have tried it, mostly regard the side effects. I have actually guessed that certain of my patients were on this diet in the past, simply by being in the same small treatment room with them. There is a distinctive odor to the breath of folks on this diet. It is not good! They notice it too.

Other side effects, taken from Dr. Atkins' books or reported by my patients who tried the diet, include the following: vitamin deficiency (assumed from the need for supplements), gas, constipation, light-headedness, grumpiness, and dry mouth (8 glasses of water are recommended each day). I have met people who have told me their cholesterol went down on this diet. Others have reported elevated cholesterol. Regardless, I doubt it's possible to reach and maintain total cholesterol levels as low as 150-160 (which I consider normal) on this diet.

Triglycerides do seem to decrease on this diet. No

surprise here. Refined carbohydrates elevate triglyceride levels. The less sugary foods eaten, the lower triglycerides tend to be. Fruits should not be considered as other sweet foods. They have a different effect than pasta or white bread or sweets would have on our blood. Dr. Atkins includes fruit in his foods to be avoided on his diet. They provide too many carbohydrates, which slow or eliminate weight loss.

My biggest concern with a diet so rich in saturated fats, while limiting the intake of other nutritious foods, is the production of blood and other cells with inferior saturated fatty acids. This will most definitely result in cells with less than optimally functioning cell membranes. This is a critical issue.

When cholesterol and triglyceride reduction is the goal, a healthy low fat diet is the best approach. If any high-fat diet were compared directly to the diet I followed in this book, there would be no question as to the blood-fat lowering champ. The low fat diet in this book will reduce cholesterol and triglycerides much faster and more completely than the high fat approach every time. By following my advice for post-cholesterol lowering, eating can be pleasurable while maintaining normal cholesterol and triglyceride levels. Most importantly, maximum levels of health will also result.

My approach also provides the added bonus of reducing other negative factors in the blood. And, unlike high fat diets, my diet does not require the addition of vitamins, minerals, and laxatives. This is a very telling fact. It is also interesting to note that a high fat diet should not be used for an extended period of time because of the imbalances it creates. A quality low fat diet can be adhered to for a lifetime with incredible health being the only side effect.

Limited Information

Those who profit from our ignorance about health have capitalized on the cholesterol situation in westernized countries. They have fed us important information about cholesterol, triglycerides, and other components of the blood. But we have been given only the information necessary to convince us to buy their products. Many of the facts we have been fed are as unhealthy as a traditional school lunch menu.

Drug manufacturers, doctors, and vegetable-spread

makers (alternatives to butter), want you believe that you need *them* to help **control** your cholesterol. They offer no **solution**. You are merely a puppet on a string, manipulated into buying their products and services for the rest of your life. This may make you wonder, are they motivated by the need to keep you healthy or by an unquenchable thirst for profits? The answer probably lies somewhere in the middle.

The large pharmaceutical companies appear to exist for profits. The sheer nature of publicly held business requires this, an unfortunate side effect of the otherwise wonderful system of free enterprise. Profits and health care are a poor mix.

To be fair, the people side of these companies likely focus on improving human health. Money is a weak long-term motivation, even in this capitalistic world. Therefore, I believe a deep seeded drive to help others motivates most health researchers.

I mention this here because I have sensed that many people have become bitter towards health care in general, and the pharmaceutical companies specifically. For all appearances, greed seems to be the motivation for the introduction of new drugs and treatments. It has been noted that pharmaceutical firms typically charge Americans many times the amount paid for drugs by people from other countries.

This fact has caused many Americans to cast a wary eye on what the drug companies do and say. They would do well to remember that once trust is lost, it is very difficult to ever regain it completely. All the warm and fuzzy TV advertising in the world will not fix the credibility issue.

The elderly population in particular has developed a deep distrust of the drug companies. That distrust also seems to be projected onto one historically unshakable relationship. By association, the industry's lust for profits has even damaged the family doctor's credibility.

Chapter VI

The Cause of High Cholesterol

What causes the increased levels of cholesterol in the blood? This is now beyond argument. Dietary excesses have been shown to directly effect total cholesterol levels in the blood. I have demonstrated this on my own blood. You can do the same.

Population studies have identified the close relationship between what you eat and the component content of your blood. You are, quite literally, what you eat. Your blood is a complex mixture of nutrients from the foods you have recently eaten, substances the body is struggling to control, and waste products from cellular metabolism. Therein lie the problem and solution to high cholesterol.

Your blood's ability to deliver nutrients to the cells of your body, *and* its ability to carry away waste products that result from the cell's metabolic processes, are *both* effected by what you eat on a daily basis. A perfect balance produced by the consumption of perfect foods results in an incredibly efficient system (once homeostasis is established). Such flawless systems can be seen readily throughout the animal kingdom where living creatures exist in an unaltered environment (not too common). It probably no longer exists within the human species, at least not in widespread fashion.

Amazing Design

The fact that humans continue to exist at all is testimony to the magnificence of our design. Our body has an absolutely spectacular ability to tolerate the incalculable stupidity that accompanies modern life. Fixing your high cholesterol, along with other "blood lipids", is the most important thing you can do to remedy this situation. Taking this one important step will put you on the path to perfect health.

Fortunately for us, He who designed our magnificent body also provided for its simple automated repair. It was built to be self-healing. Unlike the failure prone works of man, the human body is meant to provide flawless service to its owner throughout an extended lifetime.

Contrary to popular beliefs supported by modern medical philosophy, no organ is pre-programmed to "go bad" before any of the other organs. Your body is designed to work in perfect harmonious balance for a long and painless life. But, our daily habits slowly and steadily cause harm to those organs via the blood. This harm accumulates to the point at which the weak link in the chain can no longer shoulder the load.

No surprise that in America the organs most often overstressed to the point of failure are those of circulation, digestion, and filtration. The heart, gall bladder, stomach, bowel, appendix, and liver are prime candidates for surgery at some point in every American's lifetime, and probably more than once.

Did you know that in the United States over 28,000,000 surgeries are performed each and every year? The population is only around 300 million! That means that each year almost 10 percent of our population requires surgery. This is truly an embarrassment and should be a signal to our health leaders that something is drastically wrong in our health care system. Of course, the root of the problem is in our way of life.

Are you interested in discovering the simple plan that permits flawless operation of your body for a lifetime? Read on. The answer is here, I promise. You need only to read with an open mind.

Inferior Diet / Inferior Health

Most of us grew up with a diet consisting of 30-50% fat. The average American also eats 3 distinct meals every day, plus snacks. This is certainly representative of the diet most middle class kids enjoyed during a childhood in the 50's, 60's, and 70's. It was considered good nutrition at that time and sadly is still all too common in this country. Actually, as a whole, nutrition is worse!

I had wonderful parents during my childhood. They wanted to do the best for us kids. Therefore, we ate foods that the "experts" recommended. Meat and dairy products were the cornerstones of our meals. As a youth, if my mother had served a meal without some form of meat or cheese product, I would probably have cried foul! We would eat three meals each day: morning, noon, and night.

Being hungry was irrelevant. When the time came for a meal, we ate. This played an important role in the amount of sickness I have known in my life. It is no different of the rest of Americans.

In addition to watching the clock for mealtimes, we are cued to snack by gastric irritation we regularly mistake for hunger. It occurs like clockwork throughout the day. *(If Americans' bowels were as regular as our mistaken hunger pangs, no one would ever require a laxative.)* Little wonder we don't starve to death during the night by sleeping 6-8 hours without a meal!

Less Food, Better Function

Recently I walked 300 miles to Washington, DC on a fraction of the food normally eaten by Americans in an average sedentary day. During my walk I averaged 28 miles per day while consuming only 600 calories all day long. My weight loss during the trip was only about 3 pounds. I felt the best I have ever felt in my life!

I awoke at 6 AM each day, fully rested. Each day I put

in between 8 and 12 hours of walking. My diet consisted mainly of fruit, nuts, and vegetables. Though I was tired at the end of the day, I never felt weak.

My walk was an attempt to change national health care direction by meeting with congressmen. One ignored everything I said. The other, Mr. Ted Strickland listened politely for an hour. I was impressed by his attentiveness and the fact that he took an hour out of his busy day.

However, I was told that the odds of changing health care via this avenue were not good. Without any direct statement to this effect, I came away with the understanding that a snowball would have a better chance of surviving hell than any conservative approach to health care would have in Washington, DC.

Too Many Calories

Many Americans eat upwards of 2000 to 3000 calories per day! The nutrition "experts" say this is necessary for health. I believe, and science has clearly demonstrated, that this level of calories is harmful to our health. Indeed, it has been shown that regularly eating this many calories shortens our vital lifespan as well as the quality of that life. ("Beyond the 120 Year Diet" by Roy Walford, M.D.)

Let's calculate my normal energy requirement by using the "rule of 10" as recommended by the American Dietetic Association in the book, "Complete Food and Nutrition Guide" by Roberta Larson Duyff, MS, RD, CFCS. I weigh approximately 200 pounds. By the rule of 10, we multiply 200 pounds by 10 to arrive at 2000 calories required only for basic metabolism. This allows me to breathe, pump blood, and basically, survive without much extra activity.

According to the rule of 10, basic metabolism should account for about 60% of my daily calories. Therefore, my total calories for the day are recommended to be about 3,350 calories! I can tell you with total certainty that if I were to consume over 3,000 calories per day, I would soon be as big as a house. And the added stress placed on my digestive, circulatory, and respiratory systems would be devastating to my health. I know because I have lived this way during periods of my life. I was overweight and felt terrible! Premature death would be the definite outcome by continuing on this path.

The recommended daily calorie charts offered by

various other authoritative sources are equally ridiculous. The RDA (Recommended Dietary Allowances) for a man my size, 6'1", between 23 and 50 years of age, and 200 pounds would be over 3,100 calories per day. This is according to the *"Food and Nutrition Board of the National Academy of Sciences-National Research Council"*. Wow! With a title like that, it sure must be the best information available anywhere.

Still other "experts" offer complex calculations that take into account every aspect of life including daily activities, pregnancy, climate, and types of foods consumed. You name it, it's included. The attempt seems to be to categorize everyone into a small group of identifiable common traits.

Moving Target

The problem is that there is one very important fact all these techniques for calorie consumption needs miss. The calorie figure which represents basic metabolic rate is a moving target, even for the same person over time. It fluctuates with weight gain or loss, activity levels, and will change significantly with adaptation to higher or lower calorie consumption. Our diet experts try to account for this, but it is a difficult thing to do. It is quite possibly mathematically impossible.

The biggest variable, which defies measurement, is energy efficiency. Your body becomes more efficient with the consumption of different types of foods, level of calorie consumption, and changes in weight. Depending upon the quality and quantity of food consumed, your body's energy efficiency either increases or decreases. (Doesn't you car get better fuel mileage on higher octane gasoline?) How can this variation be accounted for in a generic formula? In short, it cannot.

This is a huge concept that really makes calculating basic energy requirements impossible, or at least far more complicated. Because of the high quality foods I live on, I have found that I function best on just 1,200 to 1,500 calories each day. My energy efficiency is so great that my body wastes little. By the same token it is able to thrive because it is burdened much less by unneeded extra food and the resultant waste products and byproducts of metabolism.

You may be wondering, 'Will I lose so much weight as to become thin as a toothpick?' The answer is that your body will gradually lose unnecessary and bothersome weight, but this will stop. As energy efficiency increases, the level of calories required to shed weight, drops significantly. You may have noticed this effect when attempting to lose weight. That plateau we all hit after a few weeks of rapid weight loss is accounted for by the body's increased energy efficiency.

There is magic in this process. As with all energy systems in nature, the higher the energy efficiency, the less burdensome the entire process becomes to the host. Nutrition experts would do well to learn the finer points of this phenomenon. The best way to get a feel for this process is through self-application.

What about Vitamins?

Can you get enough vitamins on a diet so low in calories? The answer is yes. It is my contention that, as energy efficiency increases with the consumption of fewer calories, so also does vitamin efficiency increase. Vitamins and minerals are used in the energy conversion processes of the body. That is to say, that they work as catalysts in all levels of digestion and assimilation of energy. It stands to reason that with less digestion and improved metabolism, there would be a reduced need for these important catalysts.

Food quality is an important factor here as well. Fruits and vegetables, nuts and seeds are the foods we are designed to draw the most value from with the least burden on the digestive system. These foods are naturally high in vitamin and mineral content relative to calorie density. That is, for the relatively low number of calories they contain, vitamin and mineral content is incredibly high. These foods provide superior nutrition without the added burden of excessive levels of foreign protein, fat, and excess calories.

I choose not to use vitamin or mineral supplements in my daily diet. I have confidence that by eating the correct foods, my nutrient needs are amply met. My diet is rich in fruits, vegetables, and nuts. I also occasionally eat seafood, perhaps two to three times per month. Less frequently, I eat some form of eggs, skim milk, or some other animal based food. These foods, which I strive to restrict in my diet, provide coverage for any concern about B vitamin deficiency, often noted as a concern in a vegetarian diet.

Negative Nutritional Factors

It is also important to understand the effect that negative factors in your diet have on vitamin and mineral balance. Coffee, tea, alcohol, cigarettes, excessive sugar intake, and refined foods, to name a few, tend to cause deficiencies of nutrients in the body. By consuming these products, you likely significantly increase the need for vitamin and mineral intake. Eliminating these negative foods from your life decreases the need for added nutrients.

Again you might be tempted to say, "In other words, if I take vitamins it's ok for me to drink and smoke, right"? This line of thinking is exactly where Americans go wrong. The body cannot be fooled into health by making up for excesses with more excesses. A price will be exacted on cheaters at some point in time. This way of reasoning opens us up to all sorts of potential pitfalls, which need to be examined by each of us individually.

We all have weaknesses. Nature does not. It responds

correctly without fail. This includes Nature's system for punishing wrong behavior. There is always a price to be paid for wrong action. That the price is not exacted at the time of wrong action accounts for our inability to recognize the connection.

In this way, we might glimpse into the reasons for increased birth defects, reduced fertility rates, and high cancer rates we see today. These genetic mistakes do not just suddenly happen. Some may be a function of genetic "traits" passed down from our parents or grandparents. I call them traits because by themselves they may not directly dictate disease. Rather, they give us the genetic predisposition toward certain illnesses. It is the influence of our daily dietary habits however, that trigger the onset of the manifestation of these ills.

This is a very deep and complex subject, too lengthy for this book. Suffice it to say that we are given here, one more reason to follow a more reasonable path in our diet and lifestyle. Our daily habits *definitely* influence genetic health traits in our family tree. All the more reason to improve those school lunches!

Food Excesses

The American diet is based upon 3 "well-rounded" meals per day. According to the new and improved food pyramid, "well-rounded" means that you should eat 6-11 servings of grains, 3-5 servings of vegetables, 2-4 servings of fruits, 2-3 servings of dairy, 2-3 servings of meats, and a sparing use of oils and sweets. It would certainly require at least 3 meals per day to fulfill those requirements! That is a whole bunch of food. Too much food in fact!

To put this into perspective, we need only consider the digestive process. After a meal, in general, digestion takes several hours depending upon the type and amount of food eaten. Fats digest much more slowly than proteins or carbohydrates. Americans eat meals that tend to be at least 30% fat. In many cases the fat content of a typical American meal may approach 50% or higher.

It is known that fat requires 3-4 hours to be released from the stomach. This is but a small part of the journey. If you live by the recommended 3 meals per day plan, your body is in a constant state of digestion during the day. This allows little time for rest or repair of the digestive tract.

And, most importantly during these hours of eating, morning till night, your blood has a constant flood of fat flowing into it.

The idea of feeling "full" by the fact that fat stays in the stomach much longer may seem helpful in say, losing weight. But the constant presence of high levels of fat in the blood slows blood flow through the capillaries. This causes a decreased flow of oxygen to all the tissues of the body. In turn, as the day progresses with more and more demands on the body and with less and less oxygen available to all the body's tissues, fatigue sets in. This accounts for the drowsy feeling you get in the afternoon. There are many important factors at work here too. This will be detailed later.

So, perhaps three meals per day are more of a drag on the body than it is helpful. But what about blood sugar? Some people have to eat more than three meals a day to keep blood sugar up, don't they? Hogwash! Fluctuating blood sugar is a sign of significant imbalance in the blood brought on by chronically poor food choices. By gradually incorporating increasing amounts of fruits and veggies in the diet, blood sugar problems disappear. This includes most cases of adult onset diabetes (Type II), a fact that is now being recognized by more and more clinical nutritionists.

You might say, "I cannot live without three meals per day, plus snacks in between." To that I say you have merely conditioned your digestive system to expect three meals per day. Fixing that problem can be difficult. Should you decide to change your eating habits by cutting down to two meals per day, you will definitely go through some discomfort for the first week or so. The result, however, is that your body will adapt to less food less frequently. A feeling of total comfort and control as you have never known can be yours if you persist. More importantly, supreme health will be your real reward. The effort is well worth the temporary discomfort.

A large portion of the stomach irritation many Americans endure day in and day out comes from a constant flow of acid into the digestive tract. This is caused by the unending influx of food and the resultant need for digestive juices. Many digestive symptoms, for which unwitting Americans rely upon medications for relief, have their root in overeating. I suffered from acid reflux and a sliding hiatus hernia for years. They both disappeared within one week of changing my diet and reducing the amount of food consumed.

You should know that it might not be necessary to cut down to two meals per day in order to reduce your cholesterol. It is likely that reduction of cholesterol levels in the blood can be achieved by merely switching to a more correct diet. The diet I relied upon to reduce my cholesterol 72 points in 3 weeks is a written record of what worked for me. I believe it would do the same for anyone. I plan to improve upon it and my general diet in the future as I continue to learn by experience.

Chapter VII

Complicating Cholesterol Matters

These days the simple idea of keeping total cholesterol under 200 mg/dl has become complicated. The ratio of good to bad cholesterol has become "more important" to many researchers. Those who manipulate facts to sell you drugs as *treatment* for your "cholesterol problem" enjoy the confusion caused by further complicating the picture. It is this author's opinion that the concept of good/bad cholesterol ratio confuses this important issue too much for the average person.

Total cholesterol is just as important to overall health and is much easier to understand. I do not dispute the importance of the different types of cholesterol. I just believe the concept of total cholesterol is easier to swallow. No pun intended! This will be discussed further at a later point in this book. For now, our discussion will focus on total cholesterol.

Resisting Change

We obviously have not been given enough incentive for reducing cholesterol in our blood. You would certainly think prevention of heart attacks and strokes would be reason enough! These two killers represent the most significant cause of premature death in America. Preventing premature death that comes decades too early seems like a good idea to me. Yet, many people choose to ignore the warnings about high cholesterol. There are various reasons for this.

Confusion stemming from misinformation about diet often causes failure and frustration in efforts to reduce cholesterol. But, refusal to give up habits known to make cholesterol remain high is probably the most common reason for not making the necessary lifestyle changes.

Many of the reasons people note in refusing to change their diet to reduce cholesterol probably mirror the reasons some give for delaying quitting smoking, despite constant pressure from doctors, family, and friends. For decades our government allowed the propagation of confusing information regarding the risks associated with cigarette smoking. This gave smokers an "out". Why quit if the evidence does not prove the health risks associated with this behavior?

I can remember a time in the 70's and 80's when our government, still caving in to the influences of the tobacco giants, did not take a strong stance against smoking. Indeed, to this day our "protectors" continue to subsidize tobacco growing, though we now know just how harmful tobacco use is. Prohibition obviously does not work, but a total ban on all advertising would help to limit the growth of this cancer in our society. Our government has been weak-kneed on this issue. Fear of offending voters has had a major impact on any real improvements in healthcare for a long, long time.

Since the government has started to enforce some rules regarding tobacco sales, smoking has begun to decline. This proves that leadership, even weak leadership, can influence people's attitudes and opinions on health issues. This gradually translates into a change in societal habits. *Imagine what a real leader could accomplish!*

I believe that confusion is the biggest reason for a less than desirable change in diet and lifestyle habits effecting cholesterol. This results from the lack of a clear message about cholesterol from our health leaders. They really need to clarify this, along with providing solid information about a diet that will result in rapid and sustained reduction of cholesterol levels. *This book is my attempt to delineate the effects that diet has had on my cholesterol levels and, if applied properly, yours too.*

Did you know that many experts do not even agree on exactly what constitutes a normal cholesterol level?

Real Change Requires Commitment

Consider this hypothetical situation. If I told you that eating less red meat *might possibly* reduce your cholesterol, would you be inclined to make that change? Not likely for most! You would be more likely to do so if I told you that eating meat ***only every other day would definitely*** reduce cholesterol in your blood to *safe* levels. It is an easy change to make, since you only have to give up red meat every other day. You could still eat chicken and fish. Also, I said nothing about sweets, alcohol, and bread. And the results are concrete. In this way you could still enjoy eating meat, but also enjoy significantly improved health. ***Remember, this is a hypothetical case. It is not true.***

This would become even more effective if I were able to convince you beyond any doubt that cholesterol reduction would *definitely* change your health for the better in some specific and recognizable way. Perhaps it would make your skin look younger, make you taller, or more virile. The more concrete the result, the more likely we are to make the effort to change. Unfortunately, the message about cholesterol has not yet been solidified to the point at which society will respond on a widespread basis.

As a side note, I can say without a doubt following a diet that corrects the American cholesterol problem definitely makes your skin younger both in appearance and in function. It also increases vigor, relieves breathing difficulties, helps us to think more clearly, and promotes a longer and more productive life. This belief I will carry to my grave as I have experienced it firsthand.

Gradual Is OK

Given the correct information, you may not change your habits completely right away. But, it would eventually become part of your consciousness, causing a gradual shift in attitude, and then an incremental change in habit. However, we need meaningful effort by our health leaders, both in government and in the private sector. Solid information that would help to motivate the general public on this issue must be promoted to a degree sufficient to cause improved levels of health.

Pharmaceutical manufacturers perpetuate rosy sounding press releases and advertising, leading us to believe statin drugs are the answer to high cholesterol. Of course these companies are constantly hyping all sorts of drugs to "treat" a wide variety of health problems. If you could only see the results of many of these drugs, you would share my outrage with each drug commercial I see on television.

A major consumer publication released a study finding that these self-anointed guardians of our health regularly promote inflated and misleading information about their drugs to doctors *and* the public. There is an ongoing effort to magnify the value of prescription drugs in our lives. You must be aware of this so that you can learn to make better decisions about the use of any drugs.

My Diet

By traditional dietetic theory, my diet is deplorable. I rarely eat breakfast and most often eat only twice a day. Three meals a day is one of those American habits that regularly undermines health. As a basic rule of thumb, I eat fruit in the morning to mid-afternoon, and then vegetables and limited grains for dinner. Since beginning to eat this way, I have enjoyed terrific energy levels, stable weight, and wonderful health. It is no accident that my total cholesterol remains below 160. All other factors of my blood are equally impressive.

Before I discovered this method of eating, I ate like every other American. Fast foods were not uncommon in my diet. Animal products were daily fare, although I rarely ate red meat over the past 20 years or so. Cheese, butter, sour cream, fried food, chicken and eggs were common. It was also common for me to eat 2,000-3,000 calories each day. I suffered the illnesses that accompany this gluttonous lifestyle as well. Over a period of fourteen years, I suffered the onset of severe springtime allergies, cold sores, fatigue, heel spurs, lethargy, periodic headaches, joint pain, and 7 *wonderful* experiences with kidney stones. Acid reflux, sweaty feet, thinning hair, fading vision, bulging gut, and poor complexion were added bonuses.

Most doctors consider these to be changes that normally accompany the aging process. But, these health problems inspired me to experiment with dietary changes such as fasting and vegetarianism, at least what I thought a vegetarian would eat. Fasting is, at times, simply miraculous. It is not, however, the answer to health problems by itself. It is also not something I would recommend for the novice except on a very limited basis. Long-term fasts can be harmful if not applied correctly. I really cannot say that I felt healthier overall with these years of dietary experiments.

Then I discovered that I had high cholesterol. I guess it really lit a fire under me to learn more about what a correct diet really is. It was a focused enough problem that I was able to find a great deal of information about it in the

National Library of Medicine, a government sponsored site on the Internet. There, the world's foremost medical research is held for our use, along with some not so great research. In general, it contains some really enlightening information.

Researchers in Denmark, Sweden, France, Japan, Germany, and Italy are far ahead of the United States with regard to dietary research. They seem more interested in the underlying cause of disease. To be fair, there are a few researchers in the US who are producing some interesting findings in calorie restriction and blood viscosity studies. *(This area of research identifies the one principle which connects most human disease processes to dietary habits.)* But as a whole, researchers only seem to be interested in this groundbreaking area of research in their quest to find a drug to artificially manipulate it. Profit is the obvious motive.

My Experiment

As a result of this research, I have experimented with

my diet over the past three years in an effort to discover the truth about the influence diet has on cholesterol. My goal was to find the perfect diet that would allow me to quickly reduce my total cholesterol. I followed a self-designed diet while having my cholesterol and triglyceride levels checked weekly. The result is that I have developed an understanding of what it takes to cause a rapid change in total blood cholesterol and triglyceride levels. The surprise was how much my total health picture improved as my blood lipid levels were reduced. I came to appreciate the connection between this and blood viscosity, the most important blood factor.

I discovered many interesting things on my journey to health. The most important seems to be a proportionate relationship between dietary changes and improvement in health. That is, the more significant the changes that you make, the more dramatic are the changes you see in blood chemistry. This made me realize how small changes in diet, as recommended by your medical doctor, often do not make perceptible changes in health, at least not in a short time.

You may look at this much in the way we look at dieting to lose weight. If you normally eat 2,500 calories/day and begin a diet of say 2,000 calories/day, the weight loss you experience will probably be minimal. Although some good things are happening in your body as a result of the slight decrease in calories, the weight loss is nearly imperceptible, as are noticeable health improvements. It really takes a significant change in total calorie intake to cause large and noticeable weight change.

This is not to say that small improvements in diet do not improve health. They do. The process is just so slow as to test the patience of a saint. Sustained over a long period of time, say years, even small improvements in diet will make dramatic positive changes in health. Of course, if you normally eat 3,000 calories of fried fatty foods per day and reduce that to 2,000 calories of the like, you will likely still die early from a heart attack or stroke. We must be realistic about the quality, as well as the degree, of improvement needed to make change.

This explains why the weak dietary recommendations of your physician often do not work. Although decreasing red meat and butter may make some change in cholesterol levels of the blood, the degree of improvement is directly proportionate to the amount of restriction you make. Your doctor is absolutely unsure exactly how much change is necessary, and he knows that he always has the statin drugs to fall back on "when" diet fails. Therefore, he errs on the side of conservatism.

Doctors Are Under Pressure

Doctors know that you do not really want to make a change in your diet. If they tell you to make drastic changes, you might choose to change doctors rather than give up the foods you love! This is bad news for your doctor. Competition for quality patients is fierce these days (i.e. good insurance, easy to work with). Unless you hold the distinction of being the biggest pain in the rear your doctor has, he wants to keep you as a patient! He knows there is always another doctor out there who is willing to tell you what you want to hear no matter if it does fall short of being the soundest advice available.

Many doctors are struggling to hang on to their patients these days. Thanks to the difficulties created by managed care and TV advertising of prescription drugs, doctors have felt increasing pressure to pacify patients by giving them what they want.

What do patients want these days? They want to have their cake and eat it too, more now than ever. They have been convinced by television "medical news" and slick print advertising written as "unbiased" medical articles that there **is** an answer for each of their health problems.

Patients sometimes think they need only find the right doctor who will provide them that magical pill, and all their health problems will abate. In fact, few if any *real* answers to health problems exist in a bottle of pills. (Don't be fooled by an experience or two where your symptoms were temporarily relieved by medication.)

Your doctor is feeling pressure from many directions to prescribe that miracle drug to "control" your cholesterol. Drug companies have been known to dangle many carrots in front of doctors to gain their allegiance.

Your doctor's family depends upon his financial success. Patients want quick and miraculous results without changing anything about their comfortable lifestyle. *(After all, this is what the drug companies have been promising us for decades. We deserve this!)* The doctor himself just wants to get through the day with limited hassles from the neurotic Mrs. Joneses of the world. Her demands have helped to make modern medical practice far too stressful.

One last challenge exists for your family doctor. Malpractice is ever looming over his or her head. Let's say your cholesterol is marginally high at 280. Your doctor puts you on a diet with even moderate success in lowering cholesterol. No drugs were prescribed. Then, although things are improving slowly, you have a heart attack.

Obviously, the protocols of the times (they are always changing) suggest that you *could have been* spared that heart attack had you been using a statin drug (probably not true). So, now you see the rock your doctor is backed up against. Who sets the protocols? Drug companies, insurance companies, and the government.

This helps to explain why your doctor's diet often does not work. It is not restrictive enough to be effective. And, the forces lined up against it can be overwhelming!

Chapter VIII

Blood Viscosity: The Root of Illness

Have you ever thought that modern health care might be far too complicated for our own good? I have. I lie awake at night thinking about it. It has occurred to me that the more detailed health sciences become, the smaller the parts they study inside our body, the further they get from the truth about health. I don't want to sound like some macrobiotic hippy or something, but truth is, simple is better.

What good is all the medical mumbo-jumbo we hear and read each day if all it accomplishes is to confuse us more? The more confused we become, the less likely we are to take action to change our health. Unless the information truly empowers us to make better decisions about the habits that control our health, it is a waste. Complicating health care serves no purpose except to enrich those who control it by our confusion.

Prescription drugs certainly fall into this category. The vast majority of medical care does also. Do you really think the medical industry wants us to be healthfully self-sufficient?

Vitamins Too!

The vitamin and herb business is another fine example. They want us to be just independent enough to buy and take their overly hyped products in an effort to stay healthy. But, who could possibly understand everything about these "miracle products"? One of the most misleading advertising schemes out there is the ploy of suggesting that some vitamin or mineral compound can relieve specific symptoms. Unscrupulous nutritional supplement pushers are bilking millions of people every day.

Most often, the people who sell these "natural miracle cures" are not very knowledgeable in the overall sense. They often sound like they know a lot about certain products. They may simply be regurgitating hype from the sales representative. Much of it may be false or misleading information, skirting the law on health claims. How can you tell if they "know" anything about that of which they speak? It's easy to become just knowledgeable enough to be dangerous.

My belief:

The more complicated an explanation is, the less confident the explainer likely is about what he is saying.

If you agree with the previous statement, or even if you don't, you are going to enjoy this chapter. I have come to the conclusion that there is one underlying and unifying cause of nearly all disease. And, it has a simple explanation.

It would be easy to close this book at this point and simply assume that I am a nut. I sincerely hope that you will not do yourself this great disservice. Hear me out. Then, if you still think me a lunatic, unable to think clearly, so be it. I will be happy to go down in history with all the other nuts, trying to change the wrong thinking of their time.

There is a high degree of order to the apparent chaos of the unhealthy body.

                                        "unknown"

Modern medicine is fond of dissecting the body down to its smallest working parts. By this method they hope to find secrets of disease. Is it possible to learn about health by studying disease? They are truly opposites.

The human body, or any living thing for that matter, is a masterpiece of engineering. Every living being consists of trillions of microscopic cells working individually, yet together as a practiced orchestra, performing the incredible symphony of life. Man could only dream of creating such a magnificent machine!

Geneticists bask in their ability to "create life" through combining an altered sperm and egg. Yet, they could do nothing if not for nature's prefabricated parts. They are mere mechanics. Science is able to do little more than to manipulate that which God has already created. I am truly embarrassed for their conceited attempt to do His work. More than that, I fear their manipulations of processes they do not fully understand, and never will. You should fear this as well!

I do not condemn scientific observation as an effort to understand. Indeed, it is from these kinds of studies that I found the truth about health. Some tremendous research has yielded real answers to the world's greatest health dilemmas. Astounding studies from countries like Denmark, Germany, Great Britain, France, and Italy can be assembled like a puzzle to create a roadmap to perfect, lasting health.

Fewer of these studies originate from our beloved United States. Why? I can only guess that the never-ending quest for a magic pill or potion has prevented research into valid prevention strategies. There is no profit to be made in prevention by natural methods. For this reason, truly important research rarely makes the news here.

The incredible research I speak of is available to anyone on the Internet in the National Library of Medicine. It is a searchable database that is a veritable treasure-trove of health information. Some knowledge of medical and scientific terminology is helpful in deciphering this information. The web address is gateway.nlm.nih.gov.

Earth Shattering Information!

So what does it say? What could be so earth shattering about it? *It defines health, that's all!* The studies I have seen describe, in tidbits here and there, how illness and disease start. With a little work, these studies come together to define the rules for a life without sickness. That's all! The most important studies deal with the effect of blood viscosity (thickness) on health. They describe the connection viscosity has to various disease processes.

In this chapter, I present the bare basics of this critical information. To go beyond the basics would fill a book itself. Understand and apply what I present here, and you can begin to enjoy real health. More detailed information about blood viscosity will appear soon. It will become the hot topic in health care when the world is ready to accept the idea that health is our own responsibility and belongs to no one else.

To begin, you must understand that every cell in your body requires delivery of oxygen and other nutrients on a constant basis in order to remain healthy. We will speak primarily of oxygen here for the sake of brevity. When oxygen flow is cutoff, the affected cells die. If this vital flow is only diminished, the cells are simply not able to function at their highest potential.

Imagine what it would be like working all day with a porous paper bag over your head, limiting your breathing to

½ of what is normal. It may not kill you, but it would definitely reduce the amount of work you could perform. You would fatigue quickly. Over the long term it would erode your health.

The process of delivering oxygen to all the cells is so critical; the body goes to great lengths to see that it is carried out as efficiently as possible. Our body is designed in such a way as to deliver oxygen to the cells no matter what activities or functions we are performing. Whether it is extremely cold, hot, dry, or raining, oxygen delivery is maintained flawlessly. If we are sitting down or running, the process continues, albeit at different rates. It is automatic, unless we interfere with it. Americans in particular are good at throwing a monkey wrench into the works. We stifle the oxygen delivery process on a daily basis.

Let's look more closely at this process. Once you have a good understanding of how oxygen delivery works and how reduction of this process makes us sick, no one can ever sell you on complicated health propaganda again.

Blood: The Miracle Fluid

Blood is the means by which the body consistently delivers oxygen to all the cells of our body. It is truly a miracle of nature. More specifically, it is the red blood cells (RBC's) within the blood that actually carry oxygen. **<u>Your body contains about 30,000 billion red blood cells!</u>** How important are RBC's to our survival? They make up *more than 99%* of all the blood cells!

RBC's are very consistent in size. They are so consistent that they are used as a comparison to determine the size of other objects under the microscope. Each RBC is approximately 7 micrometers in diameter. This fact may seem trivial to you at the moment, but it will soon become a very important clue in the mystery of good health.

Blood travels about the body through blood vessels. Nearest to the heart, these vessels are called arteries. These arteries join with smaller arterioles (small arteries), which lead to capillaries, the smallest of the vessels. Capillaries turn into venules (small veins), which then become veins. The veins connect to the heart completing the loop.

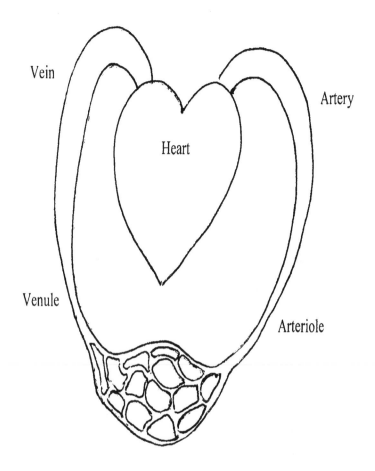

Capillary Bed

Capillaries are everywhere in the human body. No cell is more than 2 cell widths away from a capillary. Normal function here is key to good health.

It is within the capillaries that life-giving oxygen, and other nutrients, is released to the cells of the body. Once the RBC's release their oxygen to the cells, they pick up the cell's major waste product, carbon dioxide. They then travel back to the heart and lungs to dump the carbon dioxide and to pick up more oxygen. What a tremendously efficient system! Capillaries are also extremely efficient at exchanging other nutrients in the blood for cellular waste products.

The liquid part of the blood (plasma) carries these other nutrients to the cells and cellular waste products to their disposal sites, including the lungs, kidneys, and liver. In these organs, wastes are processed for reuse or disposal. There are no wasteful processes in the human body. Efficiency is the buzzword.

Capillaries, Capillaries Everywhere!

It is estimated that your body contains over 25,000 miles of capillaries! **Amazingly, this is approximately the distance around the earth at the equator!** If this fact is not startling enough, you should also know that each capillary is only about 1 millimeter long (this (-) long). So if we were to take the 40,000 million + capillaries from your body and lay them end-to-end, they would reach completely around the earth.

This seems ridiculously impossible. Yet, it is true! Does anyone want to argue the case against *Divine Design*? If so, simply explain to me how such an intricate yet simple system could ever have occurred by chance. Perhaps you could show me an example of the spontaneous generation of such complex systems in recent history.

The inside diameter of a capillary is twenty times smaller that a human hair. Capillaries may be small, but they serve a huge role in maintaining the health and integrity of the whole body.

Every cell in your body depends upon uninterrupted delivery of the blood's vital components. This has already been stated, but it bears repeating by virtue of its importance. If the blood supply is cutoff, cells die prematurely. One extreme example of this is gangrene. This often happens to diabetics because of the decreasing efficiency of circulation. As cells die from lack of oxygen in the foot for instance, the foot turns black. Another example can be seen in frostbite. Amputation is often necessary in both cases.

A less obvious example of decreased oxygen supply occurs when the blood flow is only partially diminished. This is far more common. You would be hard pressed to find an American over the age of 30 who is not effected by this problem. Symptoms can range from muscle aches and frequent colds, to fading vision or memory. It can be painful, or it can progress to more significant levels without pain.

Many diseases have their roots in this process. Here are but a few:

- Alzheimer's
- Arthritis
- Bronchitis
- Cancer
- Hair Loss
- Heart Disease
- Infections
- Osteoporosis
- Parkinson's
- Pneumonia
- Spinal-Disc Degeneration
- Stroke
- Tooth Decay
- Vision and Hearing Loss

Surprised to see infections on this list? I use it here to make a point: The point being that all illnesses may not be what they seem. Germs can only cause illness if your body's defenses are weak. Germs, which are opportunists, are present in our body at all times. Mostly they are harmless. Some germs actually help us.

Germs grow rapidly on dead and dying cells. When the oxygen supply is less than optimum, cells weaken, and some die. This creates fertile ground upon which bacteria can grow and reproduce uncontrolled. Without this rich growth medium of dead and dying cells, the body can easily hold bacteria in check. Germs are everywhere, all the time. If they were the cause of disease, why aren't we all sick all the time?

Symptoms or Simple Discomfort

Symptoms associated with decreased oxygen delivery to the cells include fatigue, muscle pain, tiredness, sexual impotence, dry skin, back pain, anxiety, excessive water weight, shortness of breath, frequent illness, and memory loss. These sound like the symptoms of aging, don't they?

The symptoms we often attribute to the aging process are actually little more than side effects of wrong living. They are also warning signs of much larger health problems to come if changes are not made quickly.

When the right changes in diet are made, a cascade of beneficial events is begun. Though these physiologic changes may be temporarily uncomfortable, they often accompany healthful changes in the body.

What kinds of changes do I speak of? The perception of hunger is one. A tired, sluggish feeling is another. Headaches are often more frequent when the body is cleaning house. Weakness may also be noticed.

Interestingly, the very kinds of symptoms we notice with illness are often present when we make good changes to our diet. Suffering through these symptoms for a week or so is a small price to pay for the kind of "rock solid health" that is the normal result.

Consistently correct diet creates health miracles!

Chapter IX

Cholesterol Connection

So what is the connection between decreased oxygen supply to the cells and high cholesterol? The answer is that the connection is a close one. The health risks associated with high cholesterol have less to do with plaque in your arteries than they do with decreasing rate of blood flow through the capillaries. These two points are intertwined.

Cholesterol plaques tend to accumulate in the large arteries and arterioles at varying rates over a lifetime. Yet, these sites of buildup cause few overt problems until they have grown so large as to block the vessel completely. This normally does not occur until our late 30's, or 40's at the earliest. Most frequently it happens even later in life. Plaques in arteries are not the roots of disease. They are merely one sign of a much deeper problem.

Capillary blood flow, on the other hand, can be reduced to the point of causing symptoms at a very young age. Children's health can be negatively affected by this problem, even in their very early years. It can make them more susceptible to infections. It most likely accounts for some of the laziness we see in teens. It is no small coincidence that today's teens tend toward a diet of highly processed, sugary, and fatty foods.

What is the cause of this problem, and what can be done about it? The capillaries themselves are not the problem. They continue to do the job they were intended for. There are plenty of them. As a matter of fact, the body produces new circulation when clogged vessels can no longer perform up to par. This can be readily seen, for example, in rheumatoid arthritis.

No, it is our old friend cholesterol, along with some of his mischievous co-conspirators, that is at the very root of this problem. Cholesterol does not act alone. His partners in crime include triglycerides, homocysteine, blood platelets, and fibrinogen.

Why the Debate?

Have you ever wondered why there is so much debate and confusion over the role that cholesterol plays in heart disease? It seems simple enough. Too much cholesterol in the blood causes heart disease. Right? But there *are* complicating factors involved.

The reason for the debate over the degree of involvement cholesterol has in heart disease and strokes is that it is only one piece of the puzzle. Too many variables make the picture fuzzy for researchers and clinicians. Some people with heart disease may not have high cholesterol.

Yet, their triglycerides or fibrinogen may be high. Because of the number of variables involved, there are many possibilities for confusion. Cholesterol is one of those variables. It is a very significant part of the problem however, and deserves a high level of focus.

All of these variables have one common root in your diet, and a similar effect on your blood health. Cholesterol, along with its partners, negatively affects blood viscosity. Mostly they are un-dissolved particles suspended in the liquid part of the blood. (Homocysteine is a chemical irritant and a byproduct of meat digestion.) The more particles floating in the blood, the thicker the blood, and the more difficult it is to pump around our body.

We can see a simple example of how increased viscosity changes the flow of liquids when we suck drinks through a straw. Water flows through a straw seemingly unimpeded. But, when we try to suck a thick milkshake through the same straw, a great deal more pressure is required. If the straw is not strong enough to withstand the pressure, it may even collapse.

Add some solid particles, like chunks of strawberry, and flow often ceases until the pressure becomes strong enough to suck the chunk through. Yet, this is not the entire picture either.

More to the Story

In order to explain the whole relationship between cholesterol and reduced capillary blood flow, we must revisit the processes that cause blood viscosity to increase. Remember that viscosity refers to the thickness of a liquid, in this case blood. But, it is not only the thickness or chunkiness of our blood that matters here. It is also important to understand processes that affect how blood cells interact with one another.

Capillaries, you may remember, are very small, 20 times smaller than a human hair. Capillaries range from 3 to 5 micrometers in diameter. As a matter of fact, capillaries are so small that you need a microscope to see them.

Red Blood Cells are larger than the capillaries through which they must pass. Difficulties arise when rbc's become rigid and sticky.

RBC size compared to a large capillary. RBC size (8 microns) is constant whereas capillaries range in size from 3 to 5 microns.

It is completely logical that capillaries are this small. Their function requires that they infiltrate every nook and cranny of the body. If they were any larger, our body size would increase exponentially. Besides, the small size of capillaries makes them ideally suited to perform their critical interactions with our cells.

Remember that red blood cells (RBC), which must pass through these tiny capillaries, are consistently about 7 micrometers in diameter. Here is a potential problem. This would seem wrong, don't you think? How could a RBC, 7 micrometers in diameter pass through a vessel that is 3 to 5 micrometers in diameter? The answer is that RBC's pass through the capillary the only way they can, one at a time.

To accomplish even this miraculous feat, they must be capable of distorting and elongating to get through these tiny openings. Flexibility is a critical aspect of the functional RBC. You can imagine that if flexibility were reduced, circulation through the capillaries would slow down significantly, possibly to a halt at times. To our gradual detriment, this is frequently the case.

Studies have demonstrated that certain components of the "Western diet" cause RBC's to become somewhat rigid.

Red blood cell membranes are partly composed of the fatty acids derived from the fat in the foods we eat. Some types of these fatty acids are better for us than others.

(Did you know that the types of fats you eat are readily identifiable by the makeup of your cellular membranes? In other words, scientists can break down your cell membranes and figure out if you have been eating beef, pork, chicken or veggies. So, we truly become exactly what we eat. No wonder some people eat like a horse!)

One More Really Sticky Problem

On top of the problem of RBC rigidity comes another significant problem. This is the problem of stickiness. The same fats that make your RBC membranes stiff also make the outer covering sticky. When RBC's are sticky, they tend to clump together. It's called RBC stacking, giving them a "rolled coin appearance."

Remember that RBC's must squeeze through capillaries one cell at a time. The rigidity presented one significant problem for capillary circulation. Now we add to that the fact that RBC's, which are stuck together, have a tough time breaking up into individual cells. This creates a compound problem for our circulation.

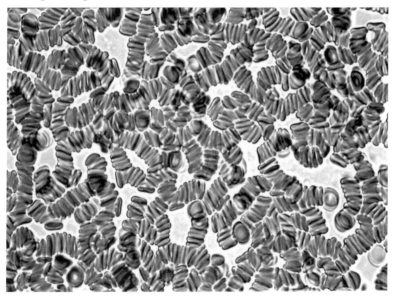

Under a microscope RBC's often have a "rouleaux" or "stacked coin" appearance. RBC's actually stick together in clumps.

The Cause/The Solution

So what is the cause of all this? Experts in this field might say the answer has to be complicated. It is, after all, a complicated problem. High cholesterol and the diseases that come with it, such as cardiovascular disease and stroke have been with us for a long time. If the answer were simple, surely science would have figured it out by now! And if that were the case no one would have high cholesterol or die from the many diseases related to it.

Right?

In my opinion, the answer *is* simple. It is so simple that it is being overlooked. Also, modern medicine is too busy making money from your sickness to solve the problem once and for all. Medical research is only interested in blood flow from the standpoint of creating new drugs to control the problem. Of course you will have to take them for the rest of your life, which will likely still be shorter than it should be.

Our government has created weak publicity programs that tiptoe around the real cause of high cholesterol and obesity. They have failed to provide us with incentives and solid information to solve this problem ourselves. You see, we are truly the only ones who can solve it. For our government your sickness has become the welfare-cause of modern times. It gives them an issue to motivate your vote for them. It also effectively makes us more dependent on the government. Talk about job security. Who would want to downsize government when we are totally dependent on the government for health care? This locks the senior citizens in tight. Fear is a strong motivator.

But, it is within our power to change this. We can correct the cause of illness in our lives. The underlying cause is in our hands to control as we choose. We must only tap into the infinite power of our will to be healthy.

To do this, to make this powerful change in our lives resulting in sweeping changes in society, we need only the **truth**. With the truth as a shield, no one need fear sickness or the dependency it creates. So far, the vast majority of the world's population does not know the truth about health and sickness. This includes many "educated" health officials.

The "Western" diet, as it is called, is full of things that cause our RBC's to clump together and lose their flexibility. It also makes normally smooth flowing, healthy blood become thick and resistant to flow. It has the propensity to rob our cells of oxygen, therefore, robbing our body of energy and life. This diet that most of us are all-too-familiar with; cheeseburgers, fries, grilled steaks, hot dogs, dairy products, and the like - is killing Americans in droves! And, it's killing our children slowly but surely.

Thanks to globalization, we have been spreading this modern form of "Black Death" to other unsuspecting citizens of the earth. Never in history have so many become wealthy on the sickness and death of so many others. But there is an answer. It is simple yet, far from easy.

Simple as 1, 2, 3

The answer is as simple as 1, 2, 3. Three components of our diet cause the vast majority of our health woes, via cholesterol elevation and associated increased blood viscosity. Through them we suffer and die. Without them we thrive. By significantly reducing them, we can live a much improved, healthful existence. The way we currently consume them, we suffer many times throughout life, then die a protracted, painful, and undignified death.

The three simple problems in our diet are...

1. **Saturated Animal Fats**

2. **Refined Sugars and Flours**

3. **Excessive Calories**

It is the regular consumption of these dietary components that undermines our health on a daily basis. It is so slow as to be imperceptible. Yet, the long-term consequences cannot be denied. The simplicity of the answer to our health problems is grand! Though simple, it is not easy. Eliminating or controlling these negative factors in our diet is difficult at best. But, the rewards are always equal to the effort, given proper time.

Remember that thing called will power? All those TV commercials selling diet pills say time and time again that you don't need it. Well, I am sorry to say that you need to sort through all the junky TV products in your closet or under your bed in order to find your will power. Drag it out and dust it off. Put a polish on it and get to know it again. You do need it. **Will power is a necessity for those who wish to be truly healthy!**

No product on earth has the power of this one tool that God gave to you for *free*. Everyone has it. We need only exercise it daily to make it strong. We must develop a deep seeded pride in our resolve. We must practice self-control!

Every easy solution man devises to sidestep the laws of nature has a tradeoff. There are no free lunches in nature. This is doubly true for matters of health. Drug and potion advertisements that claim to let you eat whatever you want and still remain slim and healthy are bogus! Accept it! Face up to it! This fact shall remain to infinity.

Prescription drugs are no different. Slick advertising offers quick solutions to problems we have embedded into our health over decades of wrong eating. They offer the hope that you can continue living your injurious lifestyle without paying the price nature has set forth as penalty for such actions. It will not work!

There are no shortcuts to supreme health. There is only a long, straight and narrow path we must follow to find our reward. The closer you stay to this path, the more secure you can be in your health. The further you stray from the path, the more profound the penalty you *will* pay during, and at the end of your physical journey.

The Path to Supreme Health

With this new understanding of health in mind, let's talk about the specific problems caused by our *3 primary negative factors*: saturated animal fats, refined sugars and flours, and excess calories.

Saturated fats (animal fats) have been implicated as the root of health problems in many studies. **(See a partial list of my references at the end of this book.)** The more saturated fats you eat, the less freely your blood can flow. Though we have the ability to digest saturated fats, we do not utilize them as well as the kind of fat that comes from plant foods. These plant foods include fruits, vegetables, nuts, seeds, berries and other things that grow from the earth.

Like other non-carnivorous animals, we are physiologically designed to eat plant foods. We are best suited to derive our nutrition from fruits, vegetables, nuts, and some seeds (plant foods). Small amounts of flesh foods can be tolerated, but only infrequently. The less frequently we eat them, the less the damage to our system.

(This book does not allow me the space to present the

lengthy argument for, and against this claim. Suffice it to say that literally everyone I have met who has given a plant-based diet more than a one month trial (with an open mind), has gushed with praise for how well they felt while eating in this manner.)

We manufacture our own saturated fats to suit the needs of our body, from the small amount of fatty acids contained in plant foods. These are uniquely qualified to serve the purposes of our body as opposed to the saturated fatty acids of cows, pigs, or chickens. Each animal has it's own specific needs.

In skipping the process of building our own saturated fats from those building blocks derived from plant sources, we are attempting to take a shortcut. By consuming meat, we choose to ingest those saturated fats that have been designed for the animals we eat. I am not a rocket scientist. This I will admit. But, I have a sneaking suspicion that the needs of cows, pigs, or chickens are somewhat different than our own. Think about it.

This makes me think of trying to put a bicycle tire on an automobile. Theoretically, both tires serve the same purpose. They are both designed to keep the vehicle suspended above the roadway for safety and smooth riding. Yet, despite the similarities, one just cannot quite replace the other. They serve the same general purpose but fill different specific requirements.

If you were to attempt to use the bicycle tire on the automobile, you would no doubt run into trouble. First off, it's unlikely the tire would fit on the rim. But even if it did, would it support the weight of a car? It may seem to work for a short time, but sooner or later there would be a price to pay. At best, the tire may blow out as soon as you let the jack down. The worst-case scenario may cost you your life.

There are likewise, penalties for trying to substitute one

kind of food where another is required. One extreme example of this is mad cow disease. This problem originated from feeding cows the desiccated remains of slaughtered animals made into a form of packaged animal chow, like dog food. This demonstrates what happens when animals, which were meant as herbivores (plant eaters), are tricked into eating meat. It is obvious that some significant line was crossed in this case.

This is a prime example of how greed caused man to attempt to circumvent Nature's laws. Man cannot even plead ignorance here. (Did you ever see a cow eating the flesh of another animal?) Besides, like the IRS, Nature does not accept ignorance as a valid excuse for breaking the law. (I don't think anyone understands either set of laws very well, IRS or Nature. Fortunately, Nature's laws are at least based on logic and common sense. And, Nature actually understands her own laws, enforcing them justly, without fail.)

My understanding of the mad cow problem is that it began as a means of making more money off cows that died before or during transport to the slaughterhouse. These are the so-called downer cattle. Sick cows, downer cattle, and the extra parts that formerly were not used from the slaughter were used to make a type of high protein food to sell back to cattle producers. It was subsequently fed to cows.

This book does not allow for a close examination of the *physiologic differences* between herbivores (example: cows), carnivores (example: cats), and omnivores (that which man is thought to be). Herbivores are grazers, eating grasses and grains primarily. Carnivores are mostly raw meat eaters. Omnivores can eat pretty much anything.

It is my opinion that these *physiological differences* leave little question as to which foods man should eat. It is sufficient to say here that this approach definitely supports my contention regarding man's natural diet. This book deals with some health outcomes of eating various foods, which certainly should be proof enough. A future book will focus upon those physiologic factors determining our ability to digest and utilize those foods efficiently.

The Saturated Fat Effect

Saturated animal fat has a known effect on our blood. Your body uses these fats to manufacture cholesterol and cell membranes. It is not necessarily the cholesterol you eat that makes your cholesterol rise. The saturated animal fats in your diet cause increased total cholesterol in your blood.

The more saturated fats you eat, the more cholesterol your body will produce. As we know, cholesterol is suspended in the blood as whole particles. Elevated cholesterol levels make our blood thicker and harder for the heart to pump around our body.

Scientific studies have also shown that consumption of these saturated fats causes our RBC's to become rigid and sticky. This happens as RBC membranes are constructed with the fatty acids obtained from the saturated animal fats in our diet. These fatty acids make our RBC membranes inferior. The results, rigidity and stickiness, are two problems that wreak havoc on our blood and health.

What about Sugars and Flours?

Refined sugars and flours have been shown to reduce the effectiveness of insulin functions in our blood. For many, the end result of this problem will be diabetes.

Diabetics as a group have blood viscosity that is higher than those without diabetes. *(Which came first, the chicken or the egg?)* Also, remember that diabetes is a known risk factor for heart disease, stroke, and many other diseases.

Keep in mind that all of these illnesses have one common cause. That is, our diet. Consumption of refined sugar and flour products can also causes extreme fluctuations of blood sugar. *Headaches, dizziness or light-headedness, false hunger, attention deficit, and mood-swings often result.*

Know anyone with any of these *"rare"* symptoms? I'll bet you do.

And Calories?

Lastly, consumption of excess calories also thickens the

blood. It should be obvious that any consumption beyond what is necessary to meet the body's daily needs forces it to deal with more supplies for, and end products of, metabolism. Extra food does not just disappear down the pipe. A normally functioning human is designed to conserve and store all calories it does not need at the moment. Excess calories are turned into fat for future use.

Regardless of their ultimate use, the consumption of food results in a forthcoming increase of triglycerides in the blood. Daily overeating will cause a sustained increase in blood triglycerides, a known threat for heart disease and stroke. *(Refined sugars and flours make eating excess calories too easy for our own good.)*

Triglycerides, like cholesterol, are a semisolid product. It is suspended in the blood in a solid particle state. Therefore, it makes the blood thicker and more difficult to pump around the body.

The Answer to Thick Blood

So now we see just what the problem is with having high cholesterol. We also now know that cholesterol is not the only culprit in the unhealthy blood of most Americans. So what is the answer? I am both sorry and happy to say that the answer to this problem is a good healthy dose of will power. It is necessary to change our diet significantly in order to effectively improve the health of our blood, and ultimately, our total health.

As long as we consume significant amounts of saturated fats, our body will continue to produce excess cholesterol. You can try to cheat nature by taking statins to reduce cholesterol while continuing to eat as you always have. This is however, a shortsighted approach. There will be a price to be paid for this shortcut at some future time.

This is like trying to dampen a fire while continuing to

feed it more wood. You can slow the fire by reducing oxygen to it, but this will result in poor burning efficiency. The end result here is a more rapid buildup of creosote in the chimney. The best way to reduce heat from the fire is to stop adding wood until it is slowed.

In order to lower cholesterol to its correct level, we must stop adding saturated fats to the body!

The diet I used to reduce my cholesterol so rapidly was very low in saturated fats. It is not easy to make the adaptation to such a tight regimen, but I assure you there is no other way. It is the right thing to do, based on the outcome.

The correctness of this approach is also obvious in the fact that, not only did cholesterol levels fall to normal, triglycerides also dropped like a rock. This was a pleasant side effect of the reduced calorie consumption that comes naturally with eating more fruits and vegetables. The body finally has a chance to use up some of the extra triglycerides that have been forever circulating as extra fuel.

This diet also undoubtedly improved other harmful components of my blood. Homocysteine (an amino acid) and fibrinogen (a plasma protein important in clotting), are important substances of the blood, but in excess are unhealthy. When an overabundance exists, they contribute to irritation of the inner lining of blood vessels and increased blood viscosity.

Although I did not have my blood tested for these factors, they undoubtedly were reduced in the process. The known factors causing elevations of these substances were removed in my diet. *Note* increased intake of folate is necessary to reduce homocysteine levels in the blood. This is naturally accomplished via increased fruit and vegetable consumption.*

Decreases in blood viscosity were evident to the naked eye. Each time my blood was drawn during the diet, a significant difference was seen in its rate of flow into the collection tube. As the viscosity decreased, flowing blood appeared more like water, and less like sludge. It certainly does not take a rocket scientist, or even a medical specialist, to recognize the benefit of this obvious change!

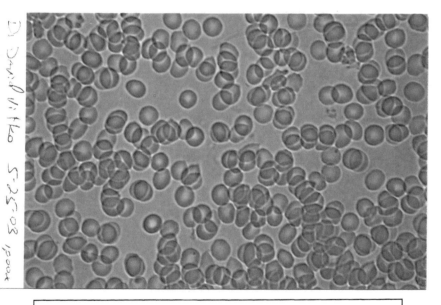

Improved diet causes newly formed RBC's to function better.
Under the microscope they often appear more independent.

Chapter X

Important Points of the Diet

If you read no other part of this book, simply following the diet will work wonders. By skipping the previous chapters, however, vital motivational information will be missed. Understanding the consequences of eating incorrectly strongly supports efforts to improve your diet. I encourage everyone to read and understand the previous chapters before or at least during the diet.

(If you would like further information about this subject, as well as other health topics, be sure to visit **concretehealth.com** on the Internet. At this site you will find more diet wisdom reflecting thinking outside of the box.)

At every meal or snack, I pause to think about how the

foods I am about to eat or drink will affect my health. This "insightful eating" is a direct result of my understanding of previously mentioned vital facts. Knowledge of these facts provides both wisdom and motivation to eat the right things on a daily basis. It does not guarantee that I will eat perfectly. I am human after all. It does help me to make better choices more often, however.

In this chapter, I will show you how you can have your health and still enjoy eating the things you love, perhaps more than ever!

Questions?

Friends and family members will ask you to explain why you are following a diet such as this. The previous chapters will give you the knowledge needed to explain your reasons for adhering to this diet. There are many. More significantly however, your answers will come from the heart with great passion. Your belief will solidify as health gradually returns to levels long since forgotten.

Stay Close

This plan is what I used to significantly and swiftly reduce my cholesterol and triglycerides. These are two heavyweights contributing to a plethora of disease processes. Although not tested for, many other important blood factors such as homocysteine, fibrinogen, uric acid, and free radicals are no doubt also improved dramatically during this diet. When the proper foods are eaten, the human body is designed to automatically correct imbalances and to promote homeostasis.

There is no way to fully understand exactly what effect may come by altering this diet as presented here. Positive results might be increased or decreased, depending on what those changes are. For instance, reducing some of the snack foods I ate during my diet likely would have accelerated the blood improvement process. Increasing consumption of these less advantageous products would slow it down. The results you receive will definitely depend upon your dedication to seeing the process through correctly.

I am not so naïve or greedy to claim that any individual food or combinations of foods in my diet have magical qualities. These are merely the foods I chose within the scope of types and amounts of foods coupled with their known physiological effects on the body. This said, there should be no assumptions made regarding the "amazing healing qualities" of any specific foods in this plan.

In recent years, science has become fond of noting

incredible individual health benefits of fiber, beta-carotene, and other minute components of certain foods. This has the unfortunate effect of bestowing "amazing healing qualities" upon carrots, beets, apples, bananas, and even chocolate bars, to name just a few, simply because they contain these "miraculous" chemical components.

All fruits, vegetables, nuts, seeds, and berries are wonderful foods. They are the foods mankind was designed to eat. But, not one of these "magical foods" in any amount can overcome the overwhelming negative effects of our daily modern diet without the elimination of those harmful foods. It is not possible to correct health problems rooted in wrong and excessive eating by adding something else to the mix. This line of thinking is wrong and continues to lead us on a futile search for a magic pill, potion, food, herb, or vitamin to cure each of our illnesses.

The real magic of natural foods lies in their daily

consumption in quantities and combinations sufficient to build rock solid health. When our daily diet is rich in life-giving fruits and vegetables, occasional indulgence of high fat or high sugar foods will have no long-term adverse effects on our health.

Therein lies the groundwork for the diet and lifestyle I know to be truly miraculous!

Hunger Versus Gastric Irritation

To reduce cholesterol and to keep it at healthy levels, some basic yet often overlooked knowledge of how our body works is absolutely essential.

We need to understand the difference between real hunger and gastric irritation. Most Americans have never experienced true hunger. We most often mistake the growling and rumbling of an unhappy belly for real hunger.

That hungry feeling which comes the morning after an evening of festive eating and drinking has little to do with true hunger. Over-eating and over-indulgence of alcoholic beverages for one evening provides enough calories to supply most people sufficient energy for *several days* of normal activities. So how is it that we perceive this as hunger? This false feeling of hunger comes to us for three reasons.

First and most significant is irritation to the stomach lining by excessive amounts of food and caustic beverages such as coffee, soda, alcohol, and tea. These cause increased amounts of acid to be produced, which reduces the pH (more acidic) to which the stomach lining is exposed over a long-term basis. This problem is the leading cause of acid reflux and hiatus hernia. (Pills and surgery are rarely needed for these problems if a real change in diet is adhered to for at least several weeks!)

Second, the false perception of hunger comes from the habitual consumption of too many calories. Habit is the operative word here. Eating too much calorie-rich food creates an expectation in our mind and stomach. If we do this too many days in a row it becomes a habit. Ending a habit can be incredibly difficult, especially when it also has a physiological component. That is, our body physically craves it.

In the quest to control my diet, changing habits has been the most successful tool I have found. For instance, if it is my habit to eat fast food while I drive, I find it impossible to reduce the number of calories I consume each day. It is far too easy to stop and order a "meal" at one of the numerous fast food joints than it is to opt for one of the few healthy choices they provide on the menu. Often times choosing one of the high fat specials appears to be a better value. Of course a high calorie drink comes with the meal. So, I might as well get a soda to go with it!

Eating fast food goes right along with eating in the car. However, if my rule is not to eat in the car, I tend to make better choices in food quality. I press myself to wait until I get home to eat. This is a great tool to help overcome poor eating habits. Besides that, it keeps the car much cleaner and smelling better.

We are not called *"creatures of habit"* for nothing. The process of ending one bad habit necessarily includes the introduction of another. Hopefully, the new habit will be a better one.

I have found that one habit helps keep me ***healthy and happy*** more than any other. This is the key to success in improving diet and, therefore, overall health.

My best good habit is to eat extremely healthfully on a daily basis, no matter the temptation. Then, twice a

month I can indulge to my heart's delight. I have found this one *good* habit helps me to conquer many other *bad* habits, while allowing me to live an incredibly enjoyable life. In addition, this is really quite rewarding psychologically. It makes me feel more in control of my life. If I fall off the wagon, as I frequently do, I need only to return to this one good habit to get straightened out in short order.

Usually, I try to plan my two indulgent days each month ahead of time. Most months allow me to plan for one special occasion like a birthday, and keep one day free for that unexpected opportunity that often arises. This would be something like a spur of the moment lunch with a friend or business associate.

The benefits of this lifestyle are numerous. Reduced weekly calorie consumption (*only 70 excess calories per week creates 1 extra pound of fat per year*), higher quality food intake, and increased satisfaction in the pleasure experienced with those two special occasions each month are but a few of the benefits. I believe this line of thinking brings us back to reality with regards to food. I look forward to dinner out much more when it comes less frequently. The idea of using food as a means of celebration loses its meaning when we over-indulge every day, as Americans often do.

The **third** and final reason for false hunger is the regular consumption of sweet, spicy, and fatty foods. Eating these kinds of foods conditions our taste buds to "always want more" of the same. Many patients have told me they do not like the taste of vegetables without copious amounts of butter, salt, or pepper. I too have found this to be true at given times of my life. The simple yet exquisite taste of fruits and vegetables cannot be appreciated when our taste buds are "burned out" from constant over-stimulation. Yet, given a proper rest, our taste buds can recover to discover hidden flavors not recognized in years!

Prove this to yourself. Get up in the morning and eat a candy bar for breakfast. During the rest of the morning ask yourself, "Do I want a piece of fruit now or more candy?" The answer will be obvious. Normally the tongue will demand foods that at least equal the flavor potency of those eaten earlier in the day.

I find that my first food of the day sets the precedent for whether I will eat healthfully or poorly until the next morning. This is a powerful tool in promoting good health.

In my less-enlightened years, I would commonly start the day with a doughnut, biscuit or snack cake, and a caffeine containing soda. I often think of those times when considering why I have suffered with so many ailments throughout my younger years. It definitely accounts for the belief that "once you hit 40 it's all downhill." Those seemingly benign daily habits of our youth are the root causes of the typical mid-life physical breakdown.

Children at Risk

The spicy/sweet food habit plays upon the health, emotions, and energy levels of our offspring too. Many children begin the day with sugar-frosted cereal, pastries, or some other poor choice for breakfast. (Anything other than fresh fruit is a poor choice.) This continues to stimulate their desire for flavorful and less-than nutritious foods throughout the rest of the day.

It also causes rapid fluctuations in blood sugar levels. Is it any wonder so many otherwise normal children are tagged as hyperactive or as having Attention Deficit Disorder these days? Their blood sugar is on an endless roller coaster ride from the time they rise in the morning until they fall into a restless sleep at the end of the day.

If children were fed some sweet yet nutritious fresh fruit for breakfast, along with a wholesome cereal or toast, most would be incredibly different in one week's time. Fruit, although sweet, has a stabilizing effect on blood sugar.

It has been a rule in our house since our children were born that breakfast is always begun with fruit. This rule has consistently served my family well in keeping our children exceedingly healthy through the years. It works equally well for adults.

Fortunately, sleep gives us a wonderful opportunity to start each day anew. A full night without food is a natural fast. It allows our body a chance to regroup and "catch-up". This works especially well if our last food is eaten four or five hours before we retire for the night. In this way, no digestive activity is needed while we sleep. Starting the day with wholesome foods sets a pattern for the entire day. Each morning presents us the opportunity to begin the re-creation of a healthy body.

Habits Revisited

A sugary breakfast habit can be a tough one to break. This is especially true when you don't particularly like your job, school, or station in life. It is easy to rationalize the need for such comfort food as a reward for our daily sacrifice of getting up and trudging off to another day of misery. Sadly, this is a self-perpetuating cycle. The more junk foods we eat, the worse we feel, the poorer we perform our job, the less satisfied we become, the more junk food we crave. Temptation is everywhere, and we truly see no benefit to self-denial. It is impossible to see the good side of any situation when we feel like crap!

This is where unfailing perseverance is required. We must believe with full conviction that a simple change in diet has the power to turn this entire situation around, because it does! The healthier we eat, the better we gradually look and feel, the better we perform our jobs, and the happier we become. As a result, more opportunities flow our way. It has the power to help us see the light in desperate situations. I have found dietary self-control to be at the very root of happiness and fulfillment.

Dietary self-control is the most powerful tool I know to lift self-esteem to its highest level!

Occasional days filled with feelings of gloom and doom that I experienced for seemingly no reason ceased to exist with a steady healthy diet.

A Price Worth Paying

With the above-mentioned points on differentiating hunger from gastric irritation, we can now look at the most difficult part of any realistic cholesterol lowering diet. I speak with total confidence in what I am saying here. Many times I have fallen off the proverbial wagon, temporarily returning to my gluttonous ways. Minor health issues always seem to bring me back to the basics. They do not appear overnight, but I have repeated this cycle enough times to know the connections are real and undeniable.

It is the habit of diet gurus to tell you what you *want* to hear. My message is the one you *must* hear in order to become truly healthy!

As I stated previously, making the adaptation to this diet can be challenging for some. I always find that I feel "hungry" for just a few days when I return to eating healthfully. *Will power is necessary here.* If I told you otherwise, I would be no better than those TV and radio snake-oil salesmen for whom I hold a great deal of contempt.

Salesmen like to manipulate the truth to fit their needs. Diet gurus have a habit of telling you what you want to hear by bending the truth. This is a feel-good tactic. It works to sell you product while the results you seek are given secondary consideration, or none at all.

I choose to give you the cold, hard truth. In this way many will decide not to follow my advice. I may alienate those who cannot hear that which does not sound pleasing or does not fit their abusive way of life. However in doing so, I know that the rewards will come without fail to those who truly seek supreme health.

Self-Denial Can Be Rewarding

I personally have come to enjoy a slightly empty feeling in my stomach. It provides a "light on my feet" feeling, which prohibits me from nothing, unlike a too-full stomach. To me, there is nothing worse than the bloated feeling I've often had after a holiday feast. Inactivity and sleep are all I am capable of when I over-indulge. This effect often lasts for days. I truly believe that many people put up with this feeling on a daily basis throughout their lives, not realizing that there is a better way.

When I have eaten very light all day, there is great pleasure in sitting down to a plate full of vegetables and rice. This pleasure is something that had been missing in my gluttonous days. Food had at times become a burden. I would wake up thinking of what flavorful mixture of "food" I would eat first. Upon completion of that meal, I would begin planning the next, and so on.

The freedom of my current style of eating is empowering! I have quantities of time that I have never had before. (Try writing a book while maintaining a busy practice or business!) Before I corrected my diet, I would be asleep on the couch in front of the TV each night by 9:30 or 10:00. When I am eating wisely, my days are long and productive without stress or struggle. Sleep requirements are reduced, indicating significantly less stress on the body.

Eat Heartily

The truth is that lowering cholesterol does not

necessitate being hungry. The foods in my diet are nutritious and very low in calories. This allows for some degree of stray from amounts listed in the menu to follow. Besides, this diet is not meant to represent a permanent way of eating. The types of foods in it are certainly beneficial over the long haul. But, the amount of food you eat may need to be manipulated in order to maintain a desired weight at the conclusion of cholesterol lowering. Also, variety is good. The key to keeping cholesterol down is to avoid animal-based foods.

Remember that cholesterol is elevated by saturated fats. As long as the main idea of primarily eating fruits and vegetables is adhered to, it is quite possible to eat until very satisfied each day while maintaining great cholesterol levels. It is also possible to keep your cholesterol levels low while being overweight. The two are only loosely connected.

A word of caution is necessary here: Increasing calorie rich foods like nuts, pastas, and grains to higher than optimum levels will have a deleterious effect on triglycerides. These often-troublesome blood fats rise with consumption of *more calories than necessary for any given day's work.* If I were going to overeat on anything in this diet, it would be vegetables. In my experience this can be done with relative impunity and will not influence weight loss. Fruits tend to have more calories than vegetables. Even moderate increases in fruit consumption beyond the amounts listed might slow weight loss.

On the other hand, if you are already very thin and would like to put a little weight on, increasing higher calorie foods slightly might be a good idea. Whole grain breads and pastas, rice, fruits, and nuts are calorie dense when compared to vegetables. By monitoring your weight each day, you can determine whether you are consuming enough, too many, or not enough calories.

Everyone's ideal weight goal will be different. I have found experience to be the best teacher with regards to the amount of food consumed. If weight is a concern, monitor it each day and alter food consumption to meet your needs. Regardless of your goals, you will find that you will be able to consume far-more food without worrying about weight gain when the majority of your diet is fruits and vegetables.

Ideal Food

It is interesting that by simply eating the foods Nature meant for us to eat, fruits and vegetables, excessive weight ceases to be a concern. There is no question that it would be difficult to become obese while subsisting on these foods. Yet, the nutrient content is considerably more substantial than a diet based on calorie-dense processed foods.

If we were really thinking, we would recognize this connection between concentrated foods of our own making and ill health. Obesity is not a disease. It is merely a sign of wrong eating. It is our body's adaptation to abnormal diet.

When we are over-weight, we are much like a fire that has had too much wood piled on it. Too much fuel makes it impossible for the fire to burn bright and hot. Oxygen delivery is stifled. The fire smolders and burns incompletely.

Fixing this problem requires withholding the addition of more fuel until the fire can consume some of the excess fuel that is already present. Poking the fire to help introduce more oxygen also helps. Once the fire begins to burn hot, small amounts of fuel can be added to maintain it.

If you think about it, there are many energy conversion

systems in our lives that are very much the same. When our automobile engine gets too much fuel, or the wrong kind of fuel, the result is a poorly performing engine. It soon gets so much carbon build-up inside that it needs major work to continue to run at all.

When it comes to energy conversion, excess fuel creates waste. The more fuel that is provided over and above that which is necessary, the poorer the energy efficiency becomes. If this sub-par energy conversion is allowed to continue unchecked, it burns itself out prematurely. For living beings, this means early and often painful death.

Exercise Is Important, but Overrated

Exercise has often been cited as means of burning extra calories and improving cholesterol. I will admit that cholesterol and triglycerides are improved by exercise. It is especially helpful in raising HDL, the good cholesterol. However, it is a deadly mistake to believe that by exercising, dietary improvement is not necessary.

More than one athlete has perished as a result of a good exercise habit coupled with poor diet. Each time I read of a highly trained athlete dying suddenly while running, I know they died unnecessarily. Eating foods rich in animal fats (average American diet) creates a dangerous unstable situation in the blood.

While writing this book, a friend who was a very well trained runner in his 50's died suddenly while on a daily run. He had minor symptoms for several weeks before this. After a thorough examination and a stress test, his doctor declared him "healthy". Sadly, this was obviously not the whole picture.

This loss has become a motivation for me to help prevent others from a similar untimely death. I keep obituaries of numerous young people who passed in their 30's, 40's, and 50's as reminders that something is just not right with our present system of health care.

My feeling is that this occurs far more commonly than any of us believe. Problems with blood viscosity are hidden from physicians because they do not have a readily available test for it. Don't fall into the trap of believing that athletes, who die suddenly, always do so because of a "hidden heart condition". The problem is most often within the blood and is totally correctable by improving the diet.

Runners would do well to adopt a healthy diet rich in fruits, veggies, nuts, berries, and the like, to complement their athletic lifestyle. The following diet is a good place to start by improving cholesterol levels and correcting numerous blood imbalances that contribute to high viscosity and sluggish blood flow.

And now, on to the diet!

Chapter XI

My Diet/My Results

On January 8, 2001 I started this diet to reduce my cholesterol. My plan was to follow a diet totally devoid of animal products. *The result was slightly less than perfect.*

I found that a few deeply ingrained habits made the total elimination of animal fats difficult. Coffee has been hard for me to give up. It is certainly not healthful and may even be harmful. But, I really enjoy it. This is especially true for coffee with cream, my favorite way to drink it.

Black coffee is probably little more than a strong irritant to the digestive tract and a neurological stimulant. Cream is primarily a saturated animal fat. Adding it to coffee certainly changes this beverage's effect on the body. (Review Chapter VIII, Blood Viscosity, The Answer to Illness, for saturated animal fat's effect on the blood.)

In the following diet, the nutritional breakdown reveals some interesting hints about the contribution that even simple habits like a morning cup of coffee, can have on our health. Compare the saturated fat content of January 11 when I returned to my coffee with cream habit, to that of January 10. Notice that the simple addition of coffee with cream accounted for a significant increase in the saturated fat content of my diet. (This, as a percentage of the RDA.)

Peanut butter also contributes to saturated fats in the diet. However, it is reasonable to assume that plant sources of saturated fats do not play a major role in elevating blood cholesterol or contributing to cholesterol-related diseases. You will note that I regularly consumed peanut butter throughout this diet, yet my cholesterol steadily dropped.

Review my blood tests carefully. You will find these tests at the beginning of each new week of daily diet notes. Notice the rapid and steady decline of total cholesterol and significant improvement in the total lipid picture. Be sure to take notice of the negative effect that one unhealthy meal had on cholesterol. (Chapter XII)   Fortunately, the body can correct for these indiscretions when they are not an every-day occurrence.

I once read a quote that went something like this: A sudden rush of water will not change a boulder, but a constant drip, drip, drip will wear the boulder away. Apply this to your diet. Eating poorly every day (drip, drip) will chisel away at your health, whereas an occasional splurge (sudden rush) will cause no major damage. (I wish I knew whom to credit for this wisdom.)

My philosophy of eating correct foods like fruits, vegetables, nuts, seeds, berries, and limited whole grains on a daily basis steadily builds health. More hazardous foods that come from animal sources should be saved for infrequent feasts, once a week or less. In this way the body has the ability to deal with the damaging effects of these foods and to return blood cholesterol to normal.

Follow this philosophy of eating and life will be good!

You alone have the power to change your health. By your actions each day you choose to strengthen or weaken your body. Every morsel of food that is placed into your mouth has either a positive or negative effect on overall health.

Every time you eat you have the opportunity to improve your health. Choose wisely at every meal.

<u>General Rules for the Menu</u>

1. Grains are measured dry and then cooked.
2. Green vegetables are interchangeable.
3. Vegetables can be added as needed to satisfy hunger.
4. Vegetables should be steamed or otherwise lightly cooked. Do not overcook!
5. Grains may be increased if weight loss is not desired.
6. Fruit may be increased by one or two pieces each day to help satisfy hunger. Any whole fruit is fine.
7. Fruits should be eaten fresh if at all possible. If fresh fruits are not available, fruit canned in water will suffice. Avoid those with added sugar.
8. Do not over-indulge on nuts unless weight gain is not a concern. They are calorie dense and will cause weight gain if taken in excess of noted amounts.
9. Listed foods can be eaten in any order, at any time of day. A preferred order might be fruits for breakfast, fruit and oatmeal for lunch, and vegetables and grains at dinner.
10. Ideally nothing should be eaten after 8 pm.
11. Potatoes must be eaten only as noted. They are calorie dense. Abuse will cause weight gain.
12. Soymilk should be substituted for skim milk if possible. (Vanilla is fantastic on oatmeal!)

Unless otherwise specified, Tests performed
███████ Health,████████Medical Center Labor
████████ Medical Park Laboratories,████████
Yo, Oh 44501. Director: ████████████ MD.

VITKO,DAVID   HOSP: ████████████
████████████   ACCT: ████████████
VITKO,DAVID M   ADM DATE: 01/08/2001

---

* L I P I D   P R O F I L E S '

01/08/01
* 1330 LIPID PROFILE
         CHOLESTEROL   ^ **221**   [<200]   MG/DL
                                        CHOLESTEROL REFERENCE RANGE:
                                        < 200   DESIRABLE
                                        200 to 239   BORDERLINE
                                        >= 240   HIGH RISK

         TRIGLYCERIDE   131   [<200]   MG/DL
                                        TRIGLYCERIDE REFERENCE RANGE:
                                        < 200   DESIRABLE
                                        200 to 399   BORDERLINE
                                        >= 400   HIGH RISK

         HDL   41   [>35]   MG/DL
                                        HDL REFERENCE RANGE:
                                        >60   DESIRABLE
                                        35 to 60   AVERAGE RISK
                                        < 35   HIGH RISK

         VERY LOW DENSITY LIPO   26   MG/DL
         LDL (CALC.)   ^ **154**   [<130]   MG/DL
                                        LDL REFERENCE RANGE:
                                        < 130   DESIRABLE
                                        130 to 159   BORDERLINE
                                        > 160   HIGH RISK

This is my initial Lipid Panel. It was drawn on the first
day of my diet. I fasted from the night before until the
blood was drawn. Each draw was performed fasting. My
weight is 216.0 pounds. It is not the focus of this study,
but is easy enough to follow out of curiosity.

Day's Diet for David M. Vitko – 01/08/01
Navel Oranges, 3 medium
Walnuts, 10-12 halves
Banana, 1 medium
Oatmeal Cereal, 2/3 cup dry
Milk, skim ½ cup
Apples, 2 medium
Brown Rice, long grain, 1 cup dry
Broccoli, 1 cup cooked
Peas, frozen, ½ cup thawed

Explanation:
Oranges and walnuts were eaten in the morning.

At lunch 2/3 cup oatmeal was measured dry, then cooked.
1 medium banana was cut up and added to the oatmeal
along with ½ cup skim milk. (Soymilk is recommended.)

Apples were peeled and sliced, eaten as a mid-afternoon
snack.

At dinner brown rice (1 cup measured dry) was cooked.
Broccoli was steamed and added to brown rice.
Frozen peas were thawed and eaten cold. (Delicious!)

Variations:
Substitute fruits that are in season.
Add a romaine lettuce salad with fat free dressing.
Peas and/or other vegetable may be added to rice.

01/08/01

Nutrient	Amount	% Of Daily Requirement
% Cal. from Fat	11.2 %	
Calories	944.4	64 %
Protein	26.62 g	48 %
Carbohydrates	196.1 g	89 %
Total Fat	12.5 g	30 %
Saturated Fat	1.3 g	9 %
Mono Fat	2.8 g	20 %
Poly Fat	6.8 g	49 %
Cholesterol	0.0 mg	0 %
Fiber	29.0 g	120 %
Caffeine	0.0 mg	0 %
Vitamin A	4159.9 RE	415 %
Vitamin C	359.7 mg	599 %
Vitamin D	0.0 IU	0 %
Vitamin E	6.6 mg	65 %
Thiamine	1.1 mg	74 %
Riboflavin	0.9 mg	53 %
Niacin	7.2 mg	37 %
Vitamin B6	1.6 mg	80 %
Vitamin B12	0.0 mcg	0 %
Folate	323.1 mcg	161 %
Sodium	412.1 mg	12 %
Calcium	501.6 mg	62 %
Magnesium	263.3 mg	75 %
Potassium	2083.5 mg	104 %
Iron	8.2 mg	82 %
Zinc	2.9 mg	19 %

Day's Diet for David M. Vitko – 01/09/01
Navel Oranges, 3 medium
Walnuts, 10-12 halves
Banana, 1 medium
Oatmeal Cereal, 2/3 cup
Milk, skim ½ cup
Apples, 2 medium
Brown Rice, long grain, 1 cup dry
Broccoli, 1 cup cooked
Peas, frozen, ½ cup thawed

Explanation:
Oranges and walnuts were eaten in the morning.

At lunch 2/3 cup oatmeal was measured dry, then cooked.
1 medium banana was cut up and added to the oatmeal
along with ½ cup skim milk. (Soymilk is recommended.)

Apples were peeled and sliced, eaten as a mid-afternoon
snack.

At dinner brown rice (1 cup measured dry) was cooked.
Broccoli was steamed and added to brown rice.
Frozen peas were thawed and eaten cold.

Variations:
Eat grapes instead of oranges. Dice apples and steep in hot
oatmeal for 3-4 minutes to add sweetness and flavor.

Remember, any fruit may be substituted for another fruit.
Be sure fruit is ripe. (Fruity aroma and sweet taste are
present.)

01/09/01

Nutrient	Amount	% Of Daily Requirement
% Cal. From Fat	11.2%	
Calories	944.4	64 %
Protein	26.62 g	48 %
Carbohydrates	196.1 g	89 %
Total Fat	12.5 g	30 %
Saturated Fat	1.3 g	9 %
Mono Fat	2.8 g	20 %
Poly Fat	6.8 g	49 %
Cholesterol	0.0 mg	0 %
Fiber	29.0 g	120 %
Caffeine	0.0 mg	0 %
Vitamin A	4159.9 RE	415 %
Vitamin C	359.7 mg	599 %
Vitamin D	0.0 IU	0 %
Vitamin E	6.6 mg	65 %
Thiamine	1.1 mg	74 %
Riboflavin	0.9 mg	53 %
Niacin	7.2 mg	37 %
Vitamin B6	1.6 mg	80 %
Vitamin B12	0.0 mcg	0 %
Folate	323.1 mcg	161 %
Sodium	412.1 mg	12 %
Calcium	501.6 mg	62 %
Magnesium	263.3 mg	75 %
Potassium	2083.5 mg	104 %
Iron	8.2 mg	82 %
Zinc	2.9 mg	19 %

Day's Diet for David M. Vitko – 01/10/01

Apples, 2 medium
Apples, 2 medium
Peanut Butter, 1 T, creamy
Bread, 2 slices whole grain/whole wheat
Orange, 1 medium
Bread, 1 slice whole grain/whole wheat
Lettuce, iceberg (1/4 head)
Dressing, 1 T, French (regular)
Sweet Potato, 1 medium baked in skin
Green Beans, canned, cooked

Explanation:

I ate 2 apples peeled and sliced in the morning.

Lunch included 2 apples peeled and sliced, along with 2 slices of toasted whole wheat bread with peanut butter.

1 orange was eaten mid-afternoon for a snack.

Salad, baked sweet potato, beans and bread for dinner.

Variations:

Other nut butter may be substituted for peanut butter in case of allergy (if able to eat safely). Almond butter is delicious!
Trade grapes or kiwi for apples.
A plain white potato is perfectly acceptable in place of the sweet potato. (no butter or sour cream)
More fruit or vegetables are OK (but not too much).

01/10/01

Nutrient	Amount	% Of Daily Requirement
% Cal. From Fat	19.4%	
Calories	1041	61 %
Protein	27.9 g	44 %
Carbohydrates	199.3 g	79 %
Total Fat	24.4 g	52 %
Saturated Fat	4.2 g	26 %
Mono Fat	9.3 g	59 %
Poly Fat	8.6 g	55 %
Cholesterol	0.0 mg	0 %
Fiber	35.9 g	149 %
Caffeine	0.0 mg	0 %
Vitamin A	2999.0 RE	299 %
Vitamin C	182.9 mg	304 %
Vitamin D	1.0 IU	0 %
Vitamin E	39.2 mg	392 %
Thiamine	1.2 mg	77 %
Riboflavin	1.0 mg	56 %
Niacin	9.4 mg	49 %
Vitamin B6	1.4 mg	69 %
Vitamin B12	0.0 mcg	0 %
Folate	770.4 mcg	385 %
Sodium	1526.5 mg	46 %
Calcium	466.7 mg	58 %
Magnesium	273.0 mg	78 %
Potassium	3344.3 mg	167 %
Iron	11.5 mg	114 %
Zinc	5.4 mg	35 %

Day's Diet for David M. Vitko – 01/11/01

Coffee, 8 oz. brewed-drip
Cream, half and half, 1 fluid oz.
Apples, 3 medium
Walnuts, 5-6 halves
Peanut Butter, ½ T
Oatmeal Cereal, ½ cup
Milk, skim, ½ cup
Oranges, navel, 2 medium
Pasta, wheat, 2 oz dry, cooked
Broccoli, Carrots, Zucchini, Summer Squash
Parmesan Cheese, grated, ¼ serving

Explanation:

Drank coffee with cream in morning. One hour later 1 apple was eaten with walnuts. (Coffee consumed with food can interfere with normal digestion.) It works like a laxative. Coffee is my *bad habit* and is not recommended!

At lunch ½ cup oatmeal was measured dry, then cooked. One apple was diced and steeped in the oatmeal. Skim milk was then added. (Soymilk is recommended.) One apple was peeled and eaten with peanut butter.
Two oranges were eaten as an afternoon snack.

At dinner whole-wheat pasta was cooked and topped with steamed vegetables of choice, then sprinkled with cheese.

Variations:

Vary the vegetables for different flavor combinations. Interchange fruits during the day. Vary nuts.

01/11/01

Nutrient	Amount	% Of Daily Requirement
% Cal. From Fat	15.0 %	
Calories	1102.5	69 %
Protein	37.8 g	63 %
Carbohydrates	211.5 g	88 %
Total Fat	19.6 g	44 %
Saturated Fat	5.6 g	37 %
Mono Fat	5.1 g	34 %
Poly Fat	6.1 g	41 %
Cholesterol	21.5 mg	13 %
Fiber	36.3 g	151 %
Caffeine	153.3 mg	61 %
Vitamin A	4370.8 RE	437 %
Vitamin C	306.6 mg	511 %
Vitamin D	80.0 IU	40 %
Vitamin E	8.3 mg	83 %
Thiamine	1.1 mg	74 %
Riboflavin	1.1 mg	67 %
Niacin	9.5 mg	50 %
Vitamin B6	2.0 mg	98 %
Vitamin B12	0.7 mcg	32 %
Folate	329.1 mcg	164 %
Sodium	375.0 mg	11 %
Calcium	770.1 mg	96 %
Magnesium	368.0 mg	105 %
Potassium	3190.8 mg	159 %
Iron	8.3 mg	82 %
Zinc	5.2 mg	34 %

Day's Diet for David M. Vitko – 01/12/01

Coffee, 8 oz. brewed-drip
Cream, half and half, ½ fluid oz.
Oranges, navel, 2 medium
Walnuts, 3-4 halves
Bread, wheat, 2 slices
Peanut Butter, ½ T
Strawberry Jam, ½ T
Baked Sweet Potato, 1 medium
Peas, canned, 1 cup

Explanation:

Drank coffee with cream in morning.
Mid-morning: peeled and snacked on 2 navel oranges with walnuts. (What a wonderful flavor combination!)

For lunch I had a peanut butter and jelly sandwich on whole grain, whole wheat bread.

At dinner I microwaved a sweet potato and heated up a cup of peas.

Variations:

Add vegetables to your satisfaction. I simply was not hungry and was satisfied with this amount of food.
Vegetables can be added and varied without changing the dietary outcome.
More fruits and nuts would be acceptable on this day as my calorie consumption was extremely low.
Interchange fruits during the day. Vary nuts.

01/12/01

Nutrient	Amount	% Of Daily Requirement
% Cal. From Fat	17.5 %	
Calories	639.0	40 %
Protein	19.2 g	32 %
Carbohydrates	115.0 g	48 %
Total Fat	12.7 g	28 %
Saturated Fat	2.6 g	17 %
Mono Fat	4.2 g	28 %
Poly Fat	4.9 g	33 %
Cholesterol	6.0 mg	3 %
Fiber	20.1 g	83 %
Caffeine	153.3 mg	61 %
Vitamin A	2688.1 RE	268 %
Vitamin C	213.3 mg	355 %
Vitamin D	11.0 IU	5 %
Vitamin E	10.1 mg	101 %
Thiamine	0.8 mg	53 %
Riboflavin	0.6 mg	34 %
Niacin	7.5 mg	39 %
Vitamin B6	0.9 mg	43 %
Vitamin B12	0.1 mcg	2 %
Folate	228.2 mcg	114 %
Sodium	1047.5 mg	31 %
Calcium	282.9 mg	35 %
Magnesium	178.0 mg	50 %
Potassium	1540.8 mg	77 %
Iron	5.1 mg	51 %
Zinc	3.1 mg	20 %

Day's Diet for David M. Vitko – 01/13/01
Honeydew Melon, ½ medium
Bread, Wheat, 2 slices
Peanut Butter, ½ T
Grape Jelly, ½ T
Oatmeal Cereal, ½ cup
Apples, 2 medium
Oranges, navel, 2 medium
Walnuts, 3-4 halves
Rice, white, 1 cup, cooked
Broccoli, Bamboo Shoots, Carrots, Celery, ½ cup each

Explanation:
Melon followed by PBJ Toast for breakfast.
Lunch included oatmeal, 1 apple steeped and 1 apple raw.
Mid-afternoon snack was oranges and walnuts.
Cooked rice topped with steamed vegetables for dinner.
(Brown rice is preferred. I ran out.)

Variations:
Add vegetables to your satisfaction. Vegetables can be
added and varied without changing the dietary outcome.
Whole-wheat spaghetti may be used in place of rice.
Interchange fruits during the day. Vary nuts.
Season all foods as desired. Use salt sparingly.

01/13/01

Nutrient	Amount	% Of Daily Requirement
% Cal. From Fat	10.1 %	
Calories	1173.8	73 %
Protein	26.8 g	45 %
Carbohydrates	252.1 g	105 %
Total Fat	14.0 g	31 %
Saturated Fat	2.1 g	14 %
Mono Fat	4.4 g	30 %
Poly Fat	5.7 g	33 %
Cholesterol	0.0 mg	0 %
Fiber	27.9 g	116 %
Caffeine	0.0 mg	0 %
Vitamin A	2145.6 RE	214 %
Vitamin C	385.2 mg	642 %
Vitamin D	6.0 IU	3 %
Vitamin E	5.6 mg	55 %
Thiamine	1.6 mg	109 %
Riboflavin	0.8 mg	45 %
Niacin	13.6 mg	71 %
Vitamin B6	1.6 mg	79 %
Vitamin B12	0.0 mcg	0 %
Folate	214.9 mcg	107 %
Sodium	1256.1 mg	38 %
Calcium	406.8 mg	50 %
Magnesium	257.7 mg	73 %
Potassium	2716.6 mg	135 %
Iron	9.0 mg	89 %
Zinc	3.6 mg	24 %

Day's Diet for David M. Vitko – 01/14/01

Coffee, 8 oz. brewed-drip
Cream, half and half, ½ fluid oz.
Milk, skim, ½ cup
Oatmeal Cereal, 2/3 cup
Apples, golden delicious, 6 medium
Bread, wheat, 2 slices
Peanut Butter, ½ T
Walnuts, 3-4 halves
Pasta, whole-wheat, 3 oz
Broccoli, Carrots, 1 cup each
Lettuce, ½ head with Catalina no-fat dressing, 2 T

Explanation:

Drank coffee with cream in morning.
Ate 2 apples with peels 2 hours later.

For lunch I ate oatmeal with 2 apples cut up and steeped,
plus 2 slices of whole-wheat toast with peanut butter.
In mid afternoon I ate 2 more apples with walnuts.

At dinner I had whole-wheat spaghetti topped with steamed
broccoli and carrots, and a head lettuce salad.

Variations:

Using a marinara sauce on the spaghetti and vegetables is
fine. (Do not use meat sauce.) Steamed mushrooms are a
tasty addition to this meal.
Use onions or peppers freely for flavor.

01/14/01

Nutrient	Amount	% Of Daily Requirement
% Cal. From Fat	11.3 %	
Calories	1405.1	88 %
Protein	39.9 g	66 %
Carbohydrates	299.7 g	125 %
Total Fat	19.3 g	43 %
Saturated Fat	3.8 g	25 %
Mono Fat	5.1 g	34 %
Poly Fat	7.0 g	47 %
Cholesterol	8.0 mg	5 %
Fiber	48.0 g	200 %
Caffeine	153.3 mg	61 %
Vitamin A	4654.1 RE	465 %
Vitamin C	189.8 mg	316 %
Vitamin D	69.0 IU	34 %
Vitamin E	10.2 mg	101 %
Thiamine	1.2 mg	80 %
Riboflavin	1.2 mg	70 %
Niacin	10.8 mg	56 %
Vitamin B6	1.9 mg	95 %
Vitamin B12	0.5 mcg	25 %
Folate	449.7 mcg	224 %
Sodium	1196.5 mg	36 %
Calcium	635.4 mg	79 %
Magnesium	340.5 mg	97 %
Potassium	3069.9 mg	153 %
Iron	13.8 mg	137 %
Zinc	5.5 mg	36 %

PAGE 1   Unless otherwise specified, Tests performed
                ⬛ Health⬛⬛⬛⬛⬛Medical Center Labor
                ⬛⬛⬛⬛⬛ Medical Park Laboratories, ⬛⬛⬛⬛
                Yo, Oh 44501. Director: ⬛⬛⬛⬛⬛⬛⬛ MD.

VITKO,DAVID   HOSP: ⬛⬛⬛⬛⬛⬛
    ⬛⬛⬛⬛⬛⬛⬛⬛   ACCT: ⬛⬛⬛⬛⬛
    VITKO,DAVID M   ADM DATE: 01/15/2001

```
* * * * * * * * * * * * * * * * * * * * * *  L I P I D    P R O F I L E S *

01/15/01
*  1240  LIPID PROFILE
           CHOLESTEROL                192      [<200]   MG/DL
                                      CHOLESTEROL REFERENCE RANGE:
                                      < 200         DESIRABLE
                                      200 to 239    BORDERLINE
                                      >= 240        HIGH RISK

           TRIGLYCERIDE               99       [<200]   MG/DL
                                      TRIGLYCERIDE REFERENCE RANGE:
                                      < 200         DESIRABLE
                                      200 to 399    BORDERLINE
                                      >= 400        HIGH RISK

           HDL                        38       [>35]    MG/DL
                                      HDL REFERENCE RANGE:
                                      >60           DESIRABLE
                                      35 to 60      AVERAGE RISK
                                      < 35          HIGH RISK

           VERY LOW DENSITY LIPO      20                MG/DL
           LDL (CALC.)              ^ 134      [<130]   MG/DL
                                      LDL REFERENCE RANGE:
                                      < 130         DESIRABLE
                                      130 to 159    BORDERLINE
                                      > 160         HIGH RISK
```

Compare these numbers to those of 01-08-01 (page
213). Notice that total cholesterol has decreased a
whopping 29 points in just one week! My body weight
is now 210.4 pounds. I have **lost 5.6 lbs** in one week.

End of Week One

The toughest week is now over. Temptations and cravings were the worst this past week. Once new eating **habits are firmly established**, it is easier to continue.

Let's look at the benefits I saw from this first week.

Blood Test Number	1	2	3	Final
Total Cholesterol	221	192		
Triglycerides	131	99		
HDL (good cholesterol)	41	38		
LDL (bad cholesterol)	154	134		
VLDL (real bad cholesterol)	26	20		

Wow! Is this great, or what? We must be onto something here. No drugs, no special herbs or vitamins, and yet everything is improving.

Is it magic? No. The reason things are improving in my blood is that I have eliminated the cause of high cholesterol. Animal fats are *the* cause. The way our body uses animal fats is different from the way it uses beneficial fats, like those from fruits, vegetables, nuts, and seeds (including grains).

The sooner we accept this fact, the sooner we can begin to make necessary changes. This will insure a long and healthy life, devoid of incapacitating illness. I choose not to end life in a nursing home. ***You?***

Day's Diet for David M. Vitko – 01/15/01

Oranges, navel, 2 medium
Walnuts, 3-4 halves
Apple, 1 medium
Tossed Salad, 3 cups
French Dressing, Catalina Fat-free, 2 T
Bread, wheat, 2 slices
Applesauce, natural, 2 T
Baked Sweet Potato, 1 medium
Green Beans, canned, 1 cup
Banana, 1 medium
Orange, 1 medium

Explanation:

For breakfast I ate two oranges with walnuts.
At 9:00 I ate an apple.

For lunch I ate a salad with mixed lettuce and dressing.
Then I ate 2 slices of toasted wheat bread with applesauce
as a topping.

Dinner was a baked sweet potato with green beans. For
desert, 2 hours later, I ate a banana and an orange.

Variations:

Add vegetables to the salad to suit your taste and to satisfy
the appetite. Vegetables can be added and varied without
changing the dietary outcome. Fresh is better than canned.
More fruits and nuts would be acceptable on this day as my
calorie consumption was extremely low.
Interchange fruits during the day. Vary nuts, or add some
peanut butter to the apple and/or banana.

01/15/01

Nutrient	Amount	% Of Daily Requirement
% Cal. From Fat	8.2 %	
Calories	817.6	51 %
Protein	18.6 g	31 %
Carbohydrates	189.9 g	79 %
Total Fat	8.2 g	18 %
Saturated Fat	1.1 g	7 %
Mono Fat	1.9 g	13 %
Poly Fat	3.9 g	26 %
Cholesterol	0.0 mg	0 %
Fiber	22.8 g	94 %
Caffeine	0.0 mg	0 %
Vitamin A	4595.5 RE	459 %
Vitamin C	335.8 mg	559 %
Vitamin D	0.0 IU	0 %
Vitamin E	11.4 mg	114 %
Thiamine	1.1 mg	72 %
Riboflavin	0.9 mg	53 %
Niacin	6.7 mg	35 %
Vitamin B6	1.8 mg	88 %
Vitamin B12	0.0 mcg	0 %
Folate	284.0 mcg	141 %
Sodium	1569.6 mg	47 %
Calcium	373.3 mg	46 %
Magnesium	219.1 mg	62 %
Potassium	2697.2 mg	134 %
Iron	6.5 mg	65 %
Zinc	3.2 mg	21 %

210

Day's Diet for David M. Vitko – 01/16/01
Banana, 1 medium
Oranges, 2 medium
Oatmeal Cereal, 2/3 cup
Apples, 2 medium
Peanut Butter, ½ T
Bread, wheat, 2 slices
Applesauce, Natural, 2 T
Pasta, wheat, 3 oz with ½ cup Marinara Sauce
Broccoli, 2 cups, Carrots, 1 cup, Mushrooms, ½ cup
Bread, wheat, 1 slice
Banana, ½ medium, Orange, 1 medium

Explanation:
I ate a banana and orange for breakfast this day. Then, at
about 10 am I had a bowl of oatmeal with a steeped apple.
While that was cooking, I ate another apple with peanut
butter.

For lunch I had 2 pieces of toast with applesauce.

Dinner consisted of wheat spaghetti topped with sauce and
lightly steamed vegetables, plus one slice of bread.
An evening snack of banana and orange was enjoyed later.

Variations:
Feel free to substitute various fruits or melon. Choose fruits
that are in season for the best flavor and nutrient value.
The oatmeal was cooked with a little additional water today
so that it could be eaten without milk.
Do not feel restricted by the times at which I ate. It really
does not matter if you change the order or meal times.

01/16/01

Nutrient	Amount	% Of Daily Requirement
% Cal. From Fat	10.6 %	
Calories	1362.3	88 %
Protein	42.0 g	72 %
Carbohydrates	284.9 g	123 %
Total Fat	17.3 g	40 %
Saturated Fat	3.0 g	20 %
Mono Fat	4.7 g	32 %
Poly Fat	5.7 g	40 %
Cholesterol	0.0 mg	0 %
Fiber	46.4 g	193 %
Caffeine	0.0 mg	0 %
Vitamin A	4611.9 RE	461 %
Vitamin C	483.4 mg	805 %
Vitamin D	8.0 IU	4 %
Vitamin E	9.9 mg	99 %
Thiamine	1.8 mg	119 %
Riboflavin	1.9 mg	108 %
Niacin	16.2 mg	85 %
Vitamin B6	3.2 mg	158 %
Vitamin B12	0.0 mcg	0 %
Folate	494.2 mcg	247 %
Sodium	1348.7 mg	40 %
Calcium	754.8 mg	94 %
Magnesium	477.1 mg	136 %
Potassium	3675.7 mg	183 %
Iron	14.0 mg	139 %
Zinc	5.2 mg	34 %

Day's Diet for David M. Vitko – 01/17/01

Oranges, navel, 2 medium
Walnuts, 3-4 halves
Oatmeal Cereal, 2/3 cup
Apples, 2 medium
Peanut Butter, ½ T
Bread, wheat, 2 slices
Applesauce, natural, 2 T
Grapefruit, 2 medium
Orange, navel, 1 medium
Popcorn, microwave plain, 1 cup
Oatmeal Cereal, 2/3 cup
Milk, skim, ½ cup

Explanation:

Breakfast included oranges and walnuts.
For lunch I had oatmeal with steeped apple and another apple with peanut butter and toast with applesauce.
At dinnertime I ate 2 grapefruits and an orange.
My evening snack was popcorn, then a bowl of oatmeal.

Variations:

Sometimes I like to eat fruit for dinner. On this day I was especially hungry after dinner. So, I chose a healthy snack in a bowl of oatmeal. (Popcorn is ok in small quantities.)
Apples are a real key to good health. Rather than an apple a day keeping the doctor away, I believe it should be 3 or 4 apples a day. (and/or other fruits)
Other "natural" cereals may suffice to replace oatmeal. The high fiber content of oatmeal is ideal for lowering cholesterol and reducing calorie consumption. It is quite filling.

01/17/01

Nutrient	Amount	% Of Daily Requirement
% Cal. From Fat	15.5 %	
Calories	1033.4	66 %
Protein	29.7 g	51 %
Carbohydrates	207.5 g	89 %
Total Fat	19.3 g	45 %
Saturated Fat	2.9 g	20 %
Mono Fat	6.5 g	45 %
Poly Fat	7.4 g	52 %
Cholesterol	2.0 mg	1 %
Fiber	23.5 g	97 %
Caffeine	0.0 mg	0 %
Vitamin A	281.0 RE	28 %
Vitamin C	423.7 mg	706 %
Vitamin D	66.0 IU	33 %
Vitamin E	6.7 mg	66 %
Thiamine	1.2 mg	79 %
Riboflavin	0.7 mg	41 %
Niacin	6.8 mg	35 %
Vitamin B6	1.2 mg	58 %
Vitamin B12	0.4 mcg	22 %
Folate	253.5 mcg	126 %
Sodium	445.3 mg	13 %
Calcium	496.8 mg	62 %
Magnesium	280.2 mg	80 %
Potassium	2372.0 mg	118 %
Iron	6.2 mg	61 %
Zinc	4.4 mg	29 %

Day's Diet for David M. Vitko – 01/18/01

Oranges, navel, 3 medium
Walnuts, 6-8 halves
Oatmeal Cereal, 2/3 cup
Milk, skim, ½ cup
Apples, 3 medium
Peanut Butter, ½ T
Cocoa, 8 fluid oz
Pasta, wheat, 2 oz
Broccoli, 1 cup, Carrots, 1 cup
Marinara Sauce, ½ cup
Parmesan Cheese, 1/8 oz grated

Explanation:

Oranges and walnuts for breakfast.
Lunch included oatmeal with milk, 1 apple steeped, and two apples eaten with peanut butter.
Early afternoon snack: Cocoa
Dinner: Spaghetti, sauce, topped with vegetables and Parmesan Cheese. (Easy on the cheese!)

Variations:

Add vegetables to your satisfaction. Onions, peppers, and mushrooms would go nicely with dinner. Vegetables can be added and varied without changing the dietary outcome.
If calorie count were not important, a slice or two of whole wheat bread would also go nicely.
Try cutting up peaches and/or bananas in your oatmeal. (Yum!)

I really started to feel significantly better today.

01/18/01

Nutrient	Amount	% Of Daily Requirement
% Cal. From Fat	19.5 %	
Calories	1375.8	89 %
Protein	45.8 g	79 %
Carbohydrates	247.6 g	107 %
Total Fat	31.6 g	73 %
Saturated Fat	9.0 g	63 %
Mono Fat	8.3 g	58 %
Poly Fat	10.1 g	70 %
Cholesterol	36.8 mg	23 %
Fiber	30.9 g	128 %
Caffeine	54.7 mg	21 %
Vitamin A	4555.1 RE	455 %
Vitamin C	378.2 mg	630 %
Vitamin D	182.0 IU	91 %
Vitamin E	8.2 mg	82 %
Thiamine	1.3 mg	83 %
Riboflavin	1.4 mg	84 %
Niacin	7.6 mg	39 %
Vitamin B6	1.8 mg	92 %
Vitamin B12	1.4 mcg	68 %
Folate	340.3 mcg	170 %
Sodium	1162.9 mg	35 %
Calcium	981 mg	122 %
Magnesium	358.3 mg	102 %
Potassium	3264.3 mg	163 %
Iron	9.0 mg	90 %
Zinc	5.2 mg	34 %

Day's Diet for David M. Vitko – 01/19/01

Bread, wheat, 2 slices
Applesauce, natural, 2 T
Oranges, navel, 2 medium
Walnuts, 6-8 halves
Oatmeal Cereal, 2/3 cup
Apples, 3 medium
Peanut Butter, ½ T
Popcorn, with oil & salt, 2 cups
Grapefruit, 2 medium

Explanation:

Breakfast consisted of 2 slices of toast with applesauce.
My mid-morning snack was peeled and separated orange
slices with walnuts, which I ate over an hour or two.

For lunch I had a bowl of oatmeal with a peeled and diced
apple steeped in it while it cooked. Two additional apples
were eaten with a thin skim of peanut butter on them.

At dinner I ate two pink grapefruits, halved and sectioned.

As a snack at about 7 pm, I had 2 cups of popcorn (2 cups
popped).

Variations:

Feel free to substitute various fruits or melon. It depends
upon what is in season. Substitute almonds or other nuts for
walnuts if you wish.
The oatmeal was cooked with a little additional water today
so that it could be enjoyed without milk.
The popcorn was a treat for week of diligent eating.

01/19/01

Nutrient	Amount	% Of Daily Requirement
% Cal. From Fat	19.6 %	
Calories	1027.8	66 %
Protein	23.8 g	41 %
Carbohydrates	200.1 g	86 %
Total Fat	24.3 g	56 %
Saturated Fat	3.3 g	23 %
Mono Fat	8.1 g	56 %
Poly Fat	10.7 g	74 %
Cholesterol	0.0 mg	0 %
Fiber	25.6 g	106 %
Caffeine	0.0 mg	0 %
Vitamin A	167.6 RE	16 %
Vitamin C	350.2 mg	583 %
Vitamin D	8.0 IU	4 %
Vitamin E	9.1 mg	91 %
Thiamine	0.9 mg	61 %
Riboflavin	0.5 mg	29 %
Niacin	6.5 mg	34 %
Vitamin B6	1.1 mg	56 %
Vitamin B12	0.0 mcg	0 %
Folate	203.4 mcg	101 %
Sodium	865.4 mg	26 %
Calcium	291.1 mg	36 %
Magnesium	251.6 mg	71 %
Potassium	2041.3 mg	102 %
Iron	5.8 mg	58 %
Zinc	4.1 mg	27 %

Day's Diet for David M. Vitko – 01/20/01

Oatmeal Cereal, 2/3 cup
Milk, skim, ¾ cup
Apples, 3 medium
Peanut Butter, ½ T
Oranges, navel, 2 medium
Bread, wheat, 1 slice
Sweet Potato, 1 medium
Salad, tossed, 3 cups

Explanation:

Oatmeal with one steeped apple and milk was breakfast
fare this day. Later in the morning 2 apples were eaten with
peanut butter.
Two oranges were eaten for lunch.
Dinner included a baked sweet potato, salad, and bread.

Variations:

All I can say about this day is that I really was not very
hungry all day. It would certainly be OK to add several
pieces of fruit and a few nuts during the day. For dinner the
addition of a vegetable or two, along with some no-fat
salad dressing, might also be considered.
You will note that the calorie count is extremely low this
day. It is interesting that some days pass without significant
desire for food. Days that find me immersed in a project of
relative importance are the easiest. ***When my thoughts are
occupied, my stomach is content to go unnoticed.***

01/20/01

Nutrient	Amount	% Of Daily Requirement
% Cal. From Fat	9.9 %	
Calories	828.0	53 %
Protein	23.8 g	41 %
Carbohydrates	177.9 g	76 %
Total Fat	9.9 g	23 %
Saturated Fat	1.8 g	12 %
Mono Fat	3.2 g	22 %
Poly Fat	2.9 g	20 %
Cholesterol	3.0 mg	1 %
Fiber	21.7 g	90 %
Caffeine	0.0 mg	0 %
Vitamin A	4609.8 RE	460 %
Vitamin C	249.8 mg	416 %
Vitamin D	83.0 IU	41 %
Vitamin E	12.1 mg	121 %
Thiamine	1.0 mg	63 %
Riboflavin	0.9 mg	51 %
Niacin	5.8 mg	30 %
Vitamin B6	1.2 mg	58 %
Vitamin B12	0.7 mcg	33 %
Folate	177.6 mcg	88 %
Sodium	325.3 mg	9 %
Calcium	501.0 mg	62 %
Magnesium	201.1 mg	57 %
Potassium	2541.2 mg	127 %
Iron	5.4 mg	54 %
Zinc	3.9 mg	25 %

Day's Diet for David M. Vitko – 01/21/01
Grapefruit, 2 pink
Walnuts, 3-4 halves
Orange, navel, 1 medium
Oatmeal Cereal, 2/3 cup
Apples, 2 medium
Peanut Butter, ½ T
Pasta, wheat, 4 oz
Sauce, Marinara, ½ cup
Broccoli, 2 cups, Carrots, 1 cup
Salad, tossed, 2 cups
Dressing, Catalina, no-fat
Bread, wheat, 1 slice

Explanation:
Breakfast: Grapefruit with walnuts.
I ate an orange for a mid-morning snack.
Lunch consisted of oatmeal with one steeped apple, plus one apple peeled and eaten with peanut butter.
For dinner I had whole-wheat spaghetti topped with a tomato sauce and a large side of steamed veggies.
Later, I ate a small salad with dressing and a slice of bread.

Variations:
Add vegetables to your satisfaction. Don't be afraid to try different combinations. That's how I discovered the tremendous flavor combination of citrus and walnuts, by pure luck. Apples and peanut butter are another treat!
You might also throw your vegetables together in a pot with a tomato broth to make a soup. Keep it all natural and don't overcook the veggies. They can lose nutrient value. Make a big pot and use it all week to save time. See the recipe in the back of this book.

01/21/01

Nutrient	Amount	% Of Daily Requirement
% Cal. From Fat	11 %	
Calories	1262.7	81 %
Protein	42.5 g	73 %
Carbohydrates	266.6 g	115 %
Total Fat	16.9 g	39 %
Saturated Fat	2.4 g	16 %
Mono Fat	4.5 g	31 %
Poly Fat	7.0 g	49 %
Cholesterol	0.0 mg	0 %
Fiber	44.0 g	183 %
Caffeine	0.0 mg	0 %
Vitamin A	5814.9 RE	581 %
Vitamin C	490.1 mg	816 %
Vitamin D	8.0 IU	4 %
Vitamin E	11.7 mg	117 %
Thiamine	1.5 mg	99 %
Riboflavin	1.4 mg	84 %
Niacin	10.9 mg	57 %
Vitamin B6	2.4 mg	117 %
Vitamin B12	0.0 mcg	0 %
Folate	396.1 mcg	198 %
Sodium	1385.8 mg	41 %
Calcium	655.9 mg	81 %
Magnesium	419.7 mg	119 %
Potassium	3288.8 mg	164 %
Iron	12.1 mg	120 %
Zinc	4.6 mg	30 %

PAGE 1   Unless otherwise specified, Tests performe
                    ████ Health.█████████ Medical Center Labo:
                    █████████ Medical Park Laboratories, ███████
                    Yo, Oh 44501. Director:██████████████ MD.

VITKO,DAVID   HOSP: ████████
    ███████████   ACCT: ████████████
    VITKO,DAVID M   ADM DATE: 01/22/2001

---

* L I P I D   P R O F I L E S

01/22/01
* 1140 LIPID PROFILE
         CHOLESTEROL   158   [<200]   MG/DL
                                     CHOLESTEROL REFERENCE RANGE:
                                     < 200   DESIRABLE
                                     200 to 239   BORDERLINE
                                     >= 240   HIGH RISK

         TRIGLYCERIDE   125   [<200]   MG/DL
                                     TRIGLYCERIDE REFERENCE RANGE:
                                     < 200   DESIRABLE
                                     200 to 399   BORDERLINE
                                     >= 400   HIGH RISK

         HDL   36   [>35]   MG/DL
                                     HDL REFERENCE RANGE:
                                     >60   DESIRABLE
                                     35 to 60   AVERAGE RISK
                                     < 35   HIGH RISK

         VERY LOW DENSITY LIPO   25   MG/DL
         LDL (CALC.)   97   [<130]   MG/DL
                                     LDL REFERENCE RANGE:
                                     < 130   DESIRABLE
                                     130 to 159   BORDERLINE
                                     > 160   HIGH RISK

Check this out. My total cholesterol has now **dropped
63 points** in just 2 weeks! This marvelous feat was
accomplished without potentially dangerous drugs.
My weight is now 208.2 pounds, **down 7.8 pounds**.

End of Week Two

At this point I am really starting to get some noticeable improvement in the way I feel. Few, who have not tried this way of eating, can understand just how good I feel about my health, my future, and life in general. It is empowering!

Here are the results at the end of week two.

Blood Test Number	1	2	3	Final
Total Cholesterol	221	192	158	
Triglycerides	131	99	125	
HDL (good cholesterol)	41	38	36	
LDL (bad cholesterol)	154	134	97	
VLDL (real bad cholesterol)	26	20	25	

Criticism will likely come from the fact that triglycerides rose slightly, as did VLDL. I offer no scientific explanation. However, it seems obvious to me by the way that I feel, that something good is happening to my blood. Remember that during house cleaning, the body has to dispose of significant garbage. Perhaps the slight rise of these negative blood factors has to do with their removal from other areas and subsequent travel through the blood on the way out. I do know that the reduction of total cholesterol is decreasing my blood viscosity and improving flow.

It may appear to you that HDL has gone down. However, the relative percentage of HDL in my blood has gone up. In week one HDL made up 19% of total cholesterol, week two 20%, and week three was 23%.

Day's Diet for David M. Vitko – 01/22/01

Coffee, 6 oz. brewed-drip
Cream, half and half, ½ fluid oz.
Apples, 2 medium
Peanut Butter, ½ T
Orange, navel, 1 medium
Walnuts, 3-4 halves
Sweet Potato, 1 medium
Baked Beans, Vegetarian, 1 cup
Bread, wheat, 2 slices
Applesauce, natural, 2 T

Explanation:

Drank coffee with cream in morning. (Old habits die hard.)
Mid-morning: peeled and snacked on 2 apples with peanut
butter.
My lunch was an orange and some walnuts.
Dinner included a baked sweet potato and baked beans.
Snack: 2 pieces of toast (whole-wheat) with applesauce

Variations:

Add more vegetables to dinner if you choose. Be creative.
Mix and match meals from other days to keep variety in
your food if you like. I actually enjoyed the simplicity of
eating basically the same foods (with small variations)
every day. Swap the sweet potato for a white potato.
If you are struggling to stay the course remember, this is
the last week. Beyond this week you can alter your diet to
enjoy an occasional splurge. Imagine how great that
unrestricted meal will taste. Savor that feeling. Use it to
your advantage. Following a plan of healthy eating with an
occasional feast will insure good health forever!

01/22/01

Nutrient	Amount	% Of Daily Requirement
% Cal. From Fat	15.1 %	
Calories	807.2	52 %
Protein	23.3 g	40 %
Carbohydrates	155.7 g	67 %
Total Fat	14.1 g	32 %
Saturated Fat	3.0 g	21 %
Mono Fat	4.8 g	33 %
Poly Fat	4.9 g	34 %
Cholesterol	6.0 mg	3 %
Fiber	18.2 g	75 %
Caffeine	115.0 mg	46 %
Vitamin A	2632.4 RE	263 %
Vitamin C	124.7 mg	207 %
Vitamin D	11.0 IU	5 %
Vitamin E	8.5 mg	84 %
Thiamine	0.9 mg	61 %
Riboflavin	0.6 mg	35 %
Niacin	7.9 mg	41 %
Vitamin B6	1.1 mg	55 %
Vitamin B12	0.1 mcg	2 %
Folate	174.4 mcg	87 %
Sodium	1325.3 mg	40 %
Calcium	336.8 mg	42 %
Magnesium	223.1 mg	63 %
Potassium	2004.8 mg	100 %
Iron	4.3 mg	43 %
Zinc	5.5 mg	36 %

Day's Diet for David M. Vitko – 01/23/01

Coffee, 6 oz. with cream, half and half, ½ fluid oz.
Oranges, navel, 3, with Walnuts, 3-4 halves
Apples, 2 medium, peanut butter, ½ T
Oatmeal Cereal, 2/3 cup
Pasta, wheat, 3 ½ oz
Broccoli, 1 ½ cup, Carrots, 1 cup, Mushrooms, ¼ cup
Sauce, marinara, ½ cup
Parmesan Cheese, 1T
Salad, tossed, 2 cups, Honey Dijon, No-fat dressing 2T
Wine, red, ¼ cup

Explanation:

Drank coffee with cream in morning. (I will quit someday!)
I ate 2 oranges with walnuts for breakfast. (I leave a
minimum of 1 hour between coffee and food.)
Mid-morning: peeled and snacked on 2 apples with peanut
butter.
My lunch was plain oatmeal and an orange.
For dinner I had spaghetti, mixed veggies, sauce and
Parmesan cheese, with a salad.
Later that evening I rewarded myself with a little red wine
and a hot bath.

Variations:

I like to keep a few different brands of spaghetti sauce
around to vary the flavor.
Salad dressings can also be varied but I tend to mostly stay
with the no-fat type.
I look for rewards other than food. For instance, a hot bath,
a purchase like a new music CD or a book are nice little
self-indulgences. (Sounds too feminine doesn't it?)

01/23/01

Nutrient	Amount	% Of Daily Requirement
% Cal. From Fat	15.9 %	
Calories	1243.7	81 %
Protein	37.9 g	65 %
Carbohydrates	233.9 g	101 %
Total Fat	22.8 g	53 %
Saturated Fat	4.8 g	34 %
Mono Fat	5.7 g	39 %
Poly Fat	8.1 g	57 %
Cholesterol	12.0 mg	7 %
Fiber	32.9 g	137 %
Caffeine	115.0 mg	46 %
Vitamin A	5927.9 RE	592 %
Vitamin C	446.9 mg	744 %
Vitamin D	19.0 IU	9 %
Vitamin E	10.7 mg	106 %
Thiamine	1.4 mg	91 %
Riboflavin	1.4 mg	82 %
Niacin	12.3 mg	64 %
Vitamin B6	2.0 mg	99 %
Vitamin B12	0.1 mcg	6 %
Folate	390.7 mcg	195 %
Sodium	1212.8 mg	36 %
Calcium	719.8 mg	89 %
Magnesium	351.8 mg	100 %
Potassium	3488.4 mg	174 %
Iron	10.8 mg	108 %
Zinc	4.5 mg	29 %

Day's Diet for David M. Vitko – 01/24/01

Grapefruit, pink, 1½ medium
Walnuts, 6-8 halves
Bread, wheat, 2 slices
Peanut Butter, 1 T
Jelly, 1T
Tea, 6 oz
Banana, 1 medium
Apples, 2 medium
Oatmeal Cereal, 2/3 cup
Milk, soy, ½ cup

Explanation:

Breakfast included grapefruit and walnuts, plus toast with peanut butter and jelly.
Later that morning I had a plain, regular cup of tea. (My misguided attempt to quit drinking coffee while still getting a little buzz.)
Lunch was a banana and two apples.
For dinner I ate a bowl of oatmeal with soymilk.

Variations:

This was a very busy day for me. I did not have much time to think about eating. Besides, I really was not very hungry. There certainly would be nothing wrong with adding some fruits and/or veggies to this day.
I wish I could explain the lack of hunger scientifically. It almost seems that my body is becoming accustomed to less fuel. I believe this is the body's adaptation to higher fuel efficiency. I know that I definitely feel more energetic despite eating less food.

01/24/01

Nutrient	Amount	% Of Daily Requirement
% Cal. From Fat	20.9 %	
Calories	936.1	54 %
Protein	25.5 g	39 %
Carbohydrates	173.0 g	67 %
Total Fat	23.3 g	48 %
Saturated Fat	2.9 g	18 %
Mono Fat	6.7 g	41 %
Poly Fat	9.8 g	61 %
Cholesterol	0.0 mg	0 %
Fiber	22.0 g	91 %
Caffeine	50.0 mg	20 %
Vitamin A	148.2 RE	14 %
Vitamin C	151.2 mg	252 %
Vitamin D	58.0 IU	29 %
Vitamin E	5.5 mg	55 %
Thiamine	0.5 mg	31 %
Riboflavin	0.5 mg	30 %
Niacin	4.1 mg	21 %
Vitamin B6	1.3 mg	66 %
Vitamin B12	1.5 mcg	75 %
Folate	86.0 mcg	42 %
Sodium	151.0 mg	4 %
Calcium	304.7 mg	38 %
Magnesium	174.2 mg	49 %
Potassium	1592.5 mg	79 %
Iron	5.5 mg	55 %
Zinc	2.7 mg	17 %

Day's Diet for David M. Vitko – 01/25/01

Coffee, 6 oz. brewed-drip
Cream, half and half, ½ fluid oz.
Banana, 3 medium, Oranges, navel, 3 medium
Walnuts, 6-8 halves
Oatmeal Cereal, 2/3 cup with soymilk, ½ cup
Apple, 1 medium, Banana, 1 medium
Peanut Butter, ½ T
Potato Chips, fat-free, 2 oz
Salad, tossed, 4 cups with fat-free dressing, 4 T
Carrots, ½ cup
Kiwi, 2 medium
Popcorn, Microwave, 2 cups

Explanation:

Drank coffee with cream in morning. One hour later ate 1 banana, 2 oranges, and walnuts.
Mid-morning snack: 1 banana
Lunch: oatmeal with banana, 1 apple with peanut butter
Afternoon snack: potato chips (fat-free), later 1 orange
For dinner I had a large salad with carrots and fat-free dressing (honey Dijon).
Evening snack: banana, kiwi, and popcorn

Variations:

Just as some days found me running away from food, others had me chasing it. I cannot explain the strong desire to eat today. Yet, I crave mostly healthy food, a good sign. To be fair, this day was full of nervous energy but not very demanding. I had a lot of time to think about food. My best days are those in which I awake with a purpose, and I set about to achieve specific goals.

01/25/01

Nutrient	Amount	% Of Daily Requirement
% Cal. From Fat	14.0 %	
Calories	1507.8	90 %
Protein	34.1 g	54 %
Carbohydrates	317.5 g	126 %
Total Fat	25.5 g	54 %
Saturated Fat	4.5 g	28 %
Mono Fat	7.0 g	44 %
Poly Fat	10.4 g	67 %
Cholesterol	6.0 mg	3 %
Fiber	33.4 g	139 %
Caffeine	115.0 mg	46 %
Vitamin A	4338.2 RE	433 %
Vitamin C	504.5 mg	840 %
Vitamin D	69.0 IU	34 %
Vitamin E	12.6 mg	126 %
Thiamine	1.4 mg	91 %
Riboflavin	1.4 mg	80 %
Niacin	9.7 mg	51 %
Vitamin B6	3.7 mg	185 %
Vitamin B12	1.5 mcg	77 %
Folate	280.6 mcg	140 %
Sodium	1318.4 mg	39 %
Calcium	583.6 mg	72 %
Magnesium	411.4 mg	117 %
Potassium	4726.2 mg	236 %
Iron	8.5 mg	85 %
Zinc	4.1 mg	27 %

Day's Diet for David M. Vitko – 01/26/01
Coffee, 6 oz. brewed-drip
Cream, half and half, ½ fluid oz.
Grapefruit, 1 medium, Walnuts, 3-4 halves
Banana, 1 medium, Apples, 2 medium
Oatmeal Cereal, 2/3 cup, Milk, soy, ½ cup
Orange, navel, 1 medium
Bread, wheat, 2 slices, Applesauce, Natural, 2 T
Angel Hair Pasta with vegetables (pre-packaged, frozen)
Popcorn, 2 cups, oil & salt
Cake, German Chocolate, 1/2 slice (1/12 of 8" cake)

Explanation:
Drank coffee with cream in morning. One hour later I ate
one grapefruit with walnuts for breakfast.
Mid-morning: I snacked on a banana.
My lunch was oatmeal with an apple steeped and soymilk. I
ate the other apple while waiting for my oatmeal to cook.
Also at lunch, I had 2 slices of toast with applesauce.
For dinner I had a commercially prepared, frozen dinner of
angel hair pasta with sauce and vegetables. (Pretty good!)
Cake was eaten reluctantly. It was my daughter's birthday
celebration. Popcorn was a late evening snack.

Variations:
The frozen dinner was actually fairly healthy. It does not
compare to fresh, raw fruits and vegetables, but is certainly
better than fatty fast foods. (Wheat pasta is better.)
The cake is a good example of how a consistently healthy
diet can allow for short excursions into deplorable eating
without much harm. I pushed this little experiment slightly
farther over the next few days.

01/26/01

Nutrient	Amount	% Of Daily Requirement
% Cal. From Fat	19.9 %	
Calories	1303.8	78 %
Protein	34.6 g	55 %
Carbohydrates	239.7 g	95 %
Total Fat	30.3 g	65 %
Saturated Fat	6.9 g	44 %
Mono Fat	10.2 g	66 %
Poly Fat	9.1 g	58 %
Cholesterol	43.5 mg	26 %
Fiber	23.6 g	98 %
Caffeine	125.1 mg	50 %
Vitamin A	441.4 RE	44 %
Vitamin C	195.6 mg	326 %
Vitamin D	69.0 IU	34 %
Vitamin E	7.6 mg	76 %
Thiamine	0.9 mg	60 %
Riboflavin	1.0 mg	59 %
Niacin	7.1 mg	37 %
Vitamin B6	1.3 mg	64 %
Vitamin B12	1.6 mcg	81 %
Folate	121.3 mcg	60 %
Sodium	1245.1 mg	37 %
Calcium	486.6 mg	60 %
Magnesium	196.3 mg	56 %
Potassium	2278.6 mg	113 %
Iron	8.7 mg	86 %
Zinc	3.0 mg	20 %

Day's Diet for David M. Vitko – 01/27/01

Grapefruit, 1 medium
Walnuts, 3-4 halves
Bread, wheat, 2 slices
Peanut Butter, 1 T, Jelly, Grape, 1 T
Apples, 2 medium
Oatmeal Cereal, 2/3 cup
Milk, soy, ½ cup
Orange, navel, 1 medium
Coffee, 6 oz. brewed-drip
Cream, half and half, ½ fluid oz.
Popcorn, cheese, 4 cups
Pasta, plain spaghetti, 3 oz, Sauce, marinara, 1 cup
Bread, Italian, 2 slices, Beer, 12 fluid oz
Salad, tossed, 1 cup with 1 T no-fat dressing

Explanation:

I ate a grapefruit, walnuts and 2 (PBJ) toast for breakfast.
For lunch I had oatmeal with soymilk and 1 apple steeped
and 1 eaten plain. I snacked on the orange after lunch.
I got carried away and gorged on cheese popcorn in the late
afternoon. (It was there and I was weak!) Coffee later.
Everything that follows was dinner out at an Italian
restaurant. (My daughter's birthday dinner.)

Variations:

This is a good example of how a birthday can pull us off
track with regard to healthy eating. This day demonstrates
my weakness and attitude shift toward eating habits. I think
I rationalized that, "Oh what the heck. I had cake last night
so now the diet is ruined. I can eat anything now."
***When we allow ourselves regular splurges this ceases to
be a problem. It removes the feeling of being deprived.***

01/27/01

Nutrient	Amount	% Of Daily Requirement
% Cal. From Fat	26.9 %	
Calories	1752.3	114 %
Protein	41.3 g	72 %
Carbohydrates	271.5 g	118 %
Total Fat	51 g	120 %
Saturated Fat	8.9 g	62 %
Mono Fat	12.1 g	85 %
Poly Fat	11.3 g	79 %
Cholesterol	41.2 mg	26 %
Fiber	28.2 g	117 %
Caffeine	115.0 mg	46 %
Vitamin A	1285.5 RE	128 %
Vitamin C	217.9 mg	363 %
Vitamin D	69.0 IU	34 %
Vitamin E	8.8 mg	87 %
Thiamine	1.0 mg	68 %
Riboflavin	1.1 mg	65 %
Niacin	14.8 mg	77 %
Vitamin B6	1.1 mg	57 %
Vitamin B12	1.7 mcg	83 %
Folate	154.8 mcg	77 %
Sodium	1638.6 mg	49 %
Calcium	477.6 mg	59 %
Magnesium	279.8 mg	77 %
Potassium	2926.3 mg	146 %
Iron	11.2 mg	111 %
Zinc	4.3 mg	28 %

Day's Diet for David M. Vitko – 01/28/01

Grapefruit, pink, 1 medium, Walnuts 3-4 halves
Apples, 2 medium, Peanut Butter, 1 T
Bread, wheat, 2 slices
Salad, tossed, 3 cups, dressing, no-fat, 2 T
Popcorn, oil & salt, 3 cups popped
Orange, navel, 2 medium
Pasta, wheat, 2 oz, Parmesan Cheese, ½ serving
Broccoli, 1 cup
Carrots, 1 cup

Explanation:

Grapefruit and Walnuts were eaten for breakfast.
My mid-morning snack was 2 golden delicious apples (my favorite) with peanut butter.
For lunch I had a tossed salad with no-fat dressing and 2 slices of whole wheat bread, plain.
Popcorn and oranges were the mid-afternoon snack today.
For dinner: whole-wheat spaghetti, broccoli, and carrots.

Variations:

Add any vegetables you choose to salads. Brown rice is a good substitute for pasta. *Couscous is one of my favorites.* Feel free to eat large salads (bigger than those described here). Just be careful not to get carried away with the dressing (even no-fat dressing). Never add eggs, meat or cheese to your salad (except on splurge day). This is one habit that can turn a healthy salad into an artery clogger!

01/28/01

Nutrient	Amount	% Of Daily Requirement
% Cal. From Fat	19.7 %	
Calories	1407.4	92 %
Protein	42.8 g	74 %
Carbohydrates	255.7 g	111 %
Total Fat	32.5 g	76 %
Saturated Fat	6.9 g	49 %
Mono Fat	11.5 g	81 %
Poly Fat	10.5 g	74 %
Cholesterol	15.0 mg	9 %
Fiber	31.0 g	129 %
Caffeine	0.0 mg	0 %
Vitamin A	6018.6 RE	601 %
Vitamin C	381.8 mg	636 %
Vitamin D	0.0 IU	0 %
Vitamin E	17.2 mg	172 %
Thiamine	1.1 mg	76 %
Riboflavin	0.9 mg	53 %
Niacin	10.7 mg	56 %
Vitamin B6	1.6 mg	80 %
Vitamin B12	0.2 mcg	10 %
Folate	273.2 mcg	136 %
Sodium	1562.6 mg	47 %
Calcium	622.8 mg	77 %
Magnesium	303.1 mg	86 %
Potassium	3017.1 mg	150 %
Iron	9.9 mg	99 %
Zinc	5.9 mg	39 %

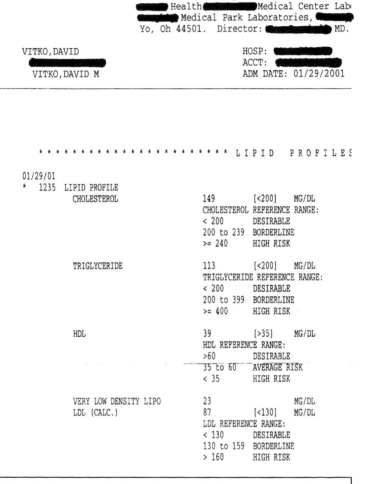

Unless otherwise specified, Tests perform▓
▓Health▓Medical Center Lab▓
▓Medical Park Laboratories, ▓
Yo, Oh 44501. Director: ▓ MD.

VITKO,DAVID

VITKO,DAVID M

HOSP: ▓
ACCT: ▓
ADM DATE: 01/29/2001

* L I P I D   P R O F I L E ▓

01/29/01
* 1235 LIPID PROFILE

```
        CHOLESTEROL              149        [<200]   MG/DL
                                 CHOLESTEROL REFERENCE RANGE:
                                 < 200          DESIRABLE
                                 200 to 239     BORDERLINE
                                 >= 240         HIGH RISK

        TRIGLYCERIDE             113        [<200]   MG/DL
                                 TRIGLYCERIDE REFERENCE RANGE:
                                 < 200          DESIRABLE
                                 200 to 399     BORDERLINE
                                 >= 400         HIGH RISK

        HDL                      39         [>35]    MG/DL
                                 HDL REFERENCE RANGE:
                                 >60            DESIRABLE
                                 35 to 60       AVERAGE RISK
                                 < 35           HIGH RISK

        VERY LOW DENSITY LIPO    23                  MG/DL
        LDL (CALC.)              87         [<130]   MG/DL
                                 LDL REFERENCE RANGE:
                                 < 130          DESIRABLE
                                 130 to 159     BORDERLINE
                                 > 160          HIGH RISK
```

Total Cholesterol has **dropped 71 points** in just 3 weeks! LDL Cholesterol (bad) is **down 67 points!** HDL (good) is down slightly (2 points) because I have not been exercising. (Easily increased by walking for ½ hour each day.) My weight is now **205.4 pounds**.

End of Week Three

The feeling of accomplishment is tremendous! I have more energy, better self-esteem, and more enthusiasm for life. For those who have gotten this far, you know what I mean. Life is too short to live with high cholesterol.

Near perfection is achieved!

Blood Test Number	1	2	3	Final
Total Cholesterol	221	192	158	**149**
Triglycerides	131	99	125	**113**
HDL (good cholesterol)	41	38	36	**39**
LDL (bad cholesterol)	154	134	97	**87**
VLDL (real bad cholesterol)	26	20	25	**23**

The improvements in my blood health are obvious. This speaks volumes about the belief that man may tolerate an omnivorous diet, but that reducing or eliminating animal products is correct, in order to produce optimum health. The proof is in the pudding.

Remember, scientists have decided proper levels of various nutrients in the human diet based upon mostly ambiguous factors. Even some very well established minimums for certain vitamins are subject to change by the removal of negative factors in the diet.

It seems to me that by adhering to a diet such as this, which produced absolutely perfect blood health, more accurate nutrient recommendations could be made.

Chapter XII

Testing the Results/Surprise!

The results speak for themselves, don't you agree? I have heard of patients reducing their total cholesterol 10 or 15 points at best by following their doctor's dietary advice. It seems extremely rare that anyone has reduced it 72 points. Not only did I reach that milestone with this diet, I did it in just 3 short weeks. And I did it without risky medications! As a bonus, I feel terrific!

Anyone who wants to be truly healthy, to become independently healthy, can do it too. All that is required is a conscious decision that *health is far more important than temporarily placating the infinite desires of our taste buds.*

"There are limits to self-indulgence, none to restraint."

Mohandas K. Gandhi
1869-1948

We must learn what is the right food for our body and shun the many foods that would harm us. We must also be wary of those who would throw us off course with temptations aimed only at increasing their own wealth.

From Monday January 29, 2001 until Saturday evening, February 3, 2001 I continued to eat as I had during the entire 3 weeks of my cholesterol-lowering diet. I had no more dietary indiscretions this week than at any other time during the previous three weeks. I was careful to remain true to myself and to those who would trust me enough to follow in my footsteps in their search for health.

Let us now see what a few tasty temptations can do to your cholesterol.

On Saturday, February 3, 2001, five days after my most recent blood work, I ate a test meal of 2 fish sandwiches, a large order of French fries, and a large cola drink. Later that evening I ate 1 cup of premium chocolate ice cream. I committed this sin against my health with full knowledge of the consequences, more or less. *I am ashamed to admit that I really enjoyed it too!*

For the entire next day, Sunday, I conformed to my healthful diet of fruits and vegetables. I then had my blood lipids tested at noon on Monday in the usual fashion.

Day's Diet for David M. Vitko – 02/03/01

Bread, wheat, 2 slices
Peanut Butter, 1 T
Strawberry Jam, 2 T
Orange, navel, 2 medium
Walnuts, 3-4 halves
Apples, 2 medium
Peanut Butter, 1 T
Bread, wheat, 1 slice
Fish Sandwich, 2 with tartar
French fries, 1 large order
Cola, 20 fluid oz
Ice Cream, chocolate, 1 cup

Explanation:

I ate toast with peanut butter and jam for breakfast.
For my mid-morning snack I had an orange with walnuts.
At lunch I had apples and toast with peanut butter.
For dinner I ate the fast food. Ice cream was desert.

Variations:

I actually ate more peanut butter today than most days. I
was not concerned about the effect it might have on my
cholesterol since I have been eating it every day while my
cholesterol continued to plummet.
Take a moment to compare the calories, total fat, saturated
fat, and nutrient content of this day to one of healthy eating,
like January 11 **(pages 198,199)**. Notice that the nutrient
count is much higher for January 11, despite the fact that
calorie consumption is only 1/3 of February 3.

02/03/01

Nutrient	Amount	% Of Daily Requirement
% Cal. From Fat	38.2 %	
Calories	3268.0	217 %
Protein	71.7 g	127 %
Carbohydrates	437.1 g	193 %
Total Fat	140.0 g	335 %
Saturated Fat	39.0 g	280 %
Mono Fat	18.8 g	134 %
Poly Fat	9.6 g	69 %
Cholesterol	200.0 mg	133 %
Fiber	15.6 g	65 %
Caffeine	84.7 mg	33 %
Vitamin A	370.1 RE	37 %
Vitamin C	180.8 mg	301 %
Vitamin D	16.0 IU	8 %
Vitamin E	6.5 mg	65 %
Thiamine	0.3 mg	22 %
Riboflavin	0.5 mg	30 %
Niacin	6.8 mg	35 %
Vitamin B6	0.6 mg	27 %
Vitamin B12	1.1 mcg	54 %
Folate	117.6 mcg	58 %
Sodium	2452.4 mg	74 %
Calcium	310.0 mg	38 %
Magnesium	150.1 mg	42 %
Potassium	1626.8 mg	81 %
Iron	7.7 mg	77 %
Zinc	4.0 mg	26 %

```
          PAGE  1              Unless otherwise specified, Tests performed
                               ████ Health.██████ Medical Center Labor
                               ███████ Medical Park Laboratories, ██████
                               Yo, Oh 44501.  Director:████████ MD.

     VITKO,DAVID                         HOSP: ██████████
     ████████████████                    ACCT: ██████████████
          VITKO,DAVID M                  ADM DATE: 02/05/2001
```

```
     * * * * * * * * * * * * * * * * * * * * * * * *  L I P I D    P R O F I L E S '

   02/05/01
   *  1330  LIPID PROFILE
            CHOLESTEROL               188        [<200]   MG/DL
                                      CHOLESTEROL REFERENCE RANGE:
                                      < 200         DESIRABLE
                                      200 to 239    BORDERLINE
                                      >= 240        HIGH RISK

            TRIGLYCERIDE            ^ 222        [<200]   MG/DL
                                      TRIGLYCERIDE REFERENCE RANGE:
                                      < 200         DESIRABLE
                                      200 to 399    BORDERLINE
                                      >= 400        HIGH RISK

            HDL                       38         [>35]    MG/DL
                                      HDL REFERENCE RANGE:
                                      >60           DESIRABLE
                                      35 to 60      AVERAGE RISK
                                      < 35          HIGH RISK

            VERY LOW DENSITY LIPO     44                  MG/DL
            LDL (CALC.)               106        [<130]   MG/DL
                                      LDL REFERENCE RANGE:
                                      < 130         DESIRABLE
                                      130 to 159    BORDERLINE
                                      > 160         HIGH RISK
```

Here is the devastating truth about the effect of high fat, sugar, and fried food. This test was performed after just one meal of fried fish and French fries. The blood test was performed 2 days after the meal. My weight is now 207.6 pounds, creeping **up 2.2 pounds**.

I knew that my total cholesterol would rise slightly. I was not prepared for how much it could rise with just one fatty meal. My total cholesterol went up 39 points!!!

This makes me all the more suspicious that for someone with already high cholesterol and triglycerides, one really fatty holiday meal could be a death sentence instead of a celebration. Blood viscosity must certainly fluctuate fairly rapidly with the influx of these fats. This would be especially true if a lot of sweets were eaten too. Sugar is well known to quickly elevate triglycerides in the blood.

I did not continue the test to determine how quickly my cholesterol dropped again with a continued healthy diet. Though the lab was aware of my study, I was told that I was abusing the privilege of testing my lipids. The medical lab did not feel it was necessary to test cholesterol "so often". "Cholesterol doesn't change that quickly", the assistant director informed me. They must have mistaken me for someone who enjoys getting stuck with needles.

Now that I can test at home, I really don't need them anymore. I'm quite confident in my **Lifestream**® home testing unit.

The significant increase in cholesterol that occurred in this test is a result of the animal fats in that one-day's diet.

Fish and French fries deep-fried in beef tallow, and milk fat in the ice cream account for this. The increase in triglycerides came from the cola and ice cream (sugar).

Notice that with this one "bad meal", my total cholesterol rose 39 points. Triglycerides went up a whopping 109 points. HDL, the "good cholesterol" went down a point. And LDL, the "bad cholesterol" went up 19 points. VLDL, the "really bad cholesterol" went up 21 points.

You may argue incorrectly that everything except triglycerides remained within normal limits. I agree that these indicators of blood health stayed within that range the "experts" consider normal. I do not consider these numbers to be normal. I believe, as do many researchers, that the "accepted numbers" are high.

However, even if these factors were within normal range, there is an important point to be learned here. Take note that all of these negative blood factors went up and remained there two days after the meal. This fact should make you realize the significance of every bite of food that you put into your mouth. **Each bite you swallow has an effect on your health, positive or negative. Nothing is neutral. No food is meaningless.**

Every Day Insult

Consider the fact that these bad changes in my blood were still present two days after the meal that caused them to rise. There is an apparent lag time for the body to deal with this influx of fats.

I presume that within hours of that fatty, sugary meal my cholesterol and other indicators spiked to a very high level. They were actually on the way down by the time I had my blood drawn a day and a half later.

What happens when you eat fatty food every day?

To continuously add fatty foods to the blood's chemical mix, without giving it a sufficient period of time to catch up and remove the bad stuff, is a recipe for disaster. We first call this disaster acute illness. Later, we fondly call it normal aging.

Let's take a look at the comparison of a good day's diet and the one I ate to screw things up.

Nutrients	01-11-01 % Of Daily Allowance	02-03-01 % Of Daily Allowance
% Calories/Fat**	15%	38.2%
Calories	69%	217%
Protein	63%	127%
Carbohydrates	88%	193%
Total Fat	44%	335%
Saturated Fat	37%	280%
Mono Fat	34%	134%
Poly Fat	41%	69%
Cholesterol	13%	133%
Fiber	151%	65%
Vitamin A	437%	37%
Vitamin C	511%	301%
Vitamin D	40%	8%
Vitamin E	83%	65%
Thiamine	74%	22%
Riboflavin	67%	30%
Niacin	50%	35%
Vitamin B6	98%	27%
Folate	164%	58%
Calcium	96%	38%
Magnesium	105%	42%
Potassium	159%	81%

** %Calories from fat is not an expression of %Daily Req.
This represents the % of calories derived from fat that day.

Conclusion

It should now be obvious that cholesterol does not have to be a problem. If you are someone with a family history of heart disease or stroke, it is imperative that you take action to lower your cholesterol immediately. Your life depends upon it.

Does this mean that you can never enjoy the taste of a steak, a baked potato with sour cream, or ice cream? No. It is quite possible to maintain excellent cholesterol levels while occasionally indulging in "less healthy" foods.

You must understand, however, that reducing elevated cholesterol to healthy levels requires a significant initial effort. Once those "perfect levels" are attained, keeping cholesterol (and other blood fats) healthy can be incredibly easy.

Establish a pattern of healthy eating on a daily basis. It is then possible to eat that fatty meal anywhere from 2 to 4 times per month. By saving these days for special occasions, the true joy of feasting as a means of celebration can once again be discovered.

Obviously, the less frequently you indulge in fatty foods, the healthier your body can become. The body can overcome intermittent lapses of over-indulgence. However, if these indiscretions become too frequent, health can quickly begin to slip away. Dietary vigilance is critical.

It is my hope that everyone can learn this new way of eating. There is no question that it represents a significant improvement over the traditional American diet.

Remember, the diet presented in this book is meant as a means of rapidly lowering cholesterol and other troublesome blood fats. The key for long-term healthy eating is to maintain a diet as free of animal fats as is humanly possible. Fruits, nuts, vegetables, and seeds (grains) should be our daily fare. Give it an honest trial for several months. I am certain that you will agree, this is the way we were meant to eat. Incredible health will be your reward.

My General Reference Sources

(The following is a partial list of books, research articles, and websites that helped me to form the opinions and beliefs I relied upon to create my cholesterol-lowering diet.)

Books:

The Holy Bible

R. C. Atkins, *Dr. Atkins' New Diet Revolution* (New York: Avon, 1999).

A. Vander, J. Sherman, D. Luciano, *Human Physiology, The Mechanisms of Body Function*, 8th Edition (New York: McGraw-Hill, 2001).

J. Whitaker, J. Roth, *Reversing Health Risks* (New York: Putnam, 1988).

H. G. Bieler, *Food Is Your Best Medicine* (New York: Random House, 1965).

R. L. Duyff, *The American Dietetic Association's Complete Food & Nutrition Guide* (Minneapolis, MN: Chronimed, 1998).

R. Walford, *Beyond The 120 Year Diet* (New York: Simon and Schuster, 2000)

***The Merck Manual, 17th Edition (New Jersey: Merck Research Laboratories, 1999).

D. Sprecher, *What You Should Know About Triglycerides* (New York: Avon, 2000).

D. Ornish, *Program For Reversing Heart Disease* (New York: Ballantine, 1990).

W. A. Price, *Nutrition And Physical Degeneration* (Santa Monica, CA: Price-Pottenger Nutrition Foundation, 1982).

B. Sears, *The Anti-Aging Zone* (New York: Regan, 1999).

Physicians' Desk Reference (PDR) 2002 Edition, (Montvale, NJ: Medical Economics Company, 2002)

Research Articles:

Wolk, A. Furuheim, M. Vessby, B. "Fatty acid composition of adipose tissue and serum lipids are valid biological markers of dairy fat intake in men." J Nutr.131(3):828-33 (2001)

Rosenson, R.S. McCormick, A Uretz, E.F. "Distribution of blood viscosity values and biochemical correlates in healthy adults." Clin Chem. Aug;42(8 Pt 1): 1189-95 (1996)

Kwok, T.K. Woo, J. Ho, S. Sham, A. "Vegetarianism and ischemic heart disease in older Chinese women." J Am Coll Nutr. Oct;19(5):622-7 (2000)

Volm, M. Mattern, J. Koomagi, R. "Inverse correlation between apoptotic (Fas ligand, caspase-3) and angiogenic factors (VEGF, microvessel desity) in squamous cell lung carcinomas." Anticancer Res May-June;19(3A):1669-71 (1999)

Barger-Lux, M.J. Heaney, R.P. "Caffeine and the calcium economy revisited." Osteoporos Int. Mar;5(2):97-102 (1995)

Williams, G.M. Williams, C.L. Weisburger, J.H. "Diet and cancer prevention: the fiber first diet." Toxicol Sci. Dec;52(2Suppl):72-86 (1999)

Carroll, S. Cooke, C.B. Butterly, R.J. "Plasma viscosity, fibrinogen and the metabolic syndrome: effect of obesity and cardiorespiratory fitness." Blood Coagul Figrinolysis Jan;11(1):71-8 (2000)

Widder, R.A. Brunner, R. Walter, P. Luke C. Bartz-Schmidt, K.U. Heimann, K. Borberg, H. "Improvement of visual acuity in patients suffering from diabetic retinopathy after membrane differential filtration: a pilot study." Trnsfus Sci. Dec;21(3):201-6 (1999)

Sandhagen, B. "Red cell fluidity in hypertension." Clin Hemorheol Microcirc 21(3-4):179-81 (1999)

Solerte, S.B. Ceresini, G. Ferrari, E. Fioravanti, M. "Hemorheological changes and overproduction of cytokines from immune cells in mild to moderate dimentia of the Alzheimer's type: adverse effects on cerebromicrovascular system." Neurobiol Aging Mar-Apr;21(2):271-81 (2001)

Knight, J.A. "The biochemistry of aging." Adv Clin Chem 35(3):1-62 (2000)

Smith, D. "Cardiovascular disease: a historic perspective." Jpn J Vet Res. 2000 Nov;48(2-3):147-66.

MacGregor, G.A. "Nutrition and blood pressure." Nutr Metab Cardiovasc Dis. 1999 Aug;9(4Suppl):6-15.

Sloop, G.D., Mercante, D.E. "Opposite effects of low-density lipoprotein on blood viscosity in fasting subjects." Clin Hemorheol Microcirc 1998 Nov;19(3):197-203.

Other Sources:

American Heart Association, *www.americanheart.org*

Diamond Walnuts, *www.diamondwalnut.com*

Information on cellular membrane structure and function, *www.cytochemistry.net*

Government sponsored information and health studies, *www.health.gov*

Home Cholesterol testing, *www.KnowItForLife.com* or *www.lifestreamtech.com*

Favorite Healthy Recipe
(It tastes great too!)

The problem with healthy eating is that most people think the food tastes bland. Well don't forget what I said about your taste buds being burned out from fatty and spicy foods. One day without food, just water (a short fast) does wonders to restore an appreciation for the less-dramatic flavors found in fruits and vegetables.

Of course, you can also accomplish this improvement by simply eating less frequently and sticking with a healthy diet for several weeks. I tend to stay with foods that require no cooking. But, here is a recipe that satisfies my desire for spicy food without the fat. It is especially good in colder weather.

Vegetable Soup

Cook down 8-10 medium sized tomatoes (or use canned tomatoes). Remove the skins and seeds if you prefer by straining them through a colander. Simmer juice for ½ hour or more with 2 cloves garlic and/or diced onion.

Add ½ cup of barley, bulgar wheat, or brown rice. Then add 1 cup peas, 1-2 medium zucchini (cut into medium sized cubes), 1 cup carrots, and 6-8 diced mushrooms. Cook until grain is fully cooked (about ½ hour). You may season as desired with salt and pepper. Enjoy!

Alternatives: Use cabbage instead of/or in addition to onion and garlic. Potatoes may also be substituted for grain. (This recipe can be altered in many ways to suit your taste.) Don't be afraid to experiment. Make a big pot if you like it, and store it in the refrigerator to enjoy all week.

Order Pages:

Do you see the logic in Dr. Vitko's way of thinking about health? Then you may by interested in owning one or more of his informative and highly motivational tapes or CD's. Dr. David Vitko brings forth his enthusiasm for the "Truth about health" in these exciting recordings and his live lecture series.

If you are tired of lies and broken promises when it comes to your health, you need to hear this "Rock Solid Health" information. There **is** a very real solution to your health problems. But, it does not come in a bottle, vitamin, pill, or potion. These "treatments" can do little more than cover up symptoms. Remember that **incredible health is free** to anyone who makes the effort to learn and apply Nature's laws. The answers do come to those who truly seek them.

Find the answer you seek in the products that follow.

Current Products and Price List

3 Weeks To Perfect Cholesterol (without drugs!) The terrific book which explains the Truth about cholesterol. ……. **only $24.95**

Enjoy Incredible Health, Dr. Vitko's original motivational health audio recording. Available in cassette tape or CD (approx 1 hour in length**).… $9.95**

Supercharge Your Vitamins and Your Health, This audio recording could make the difference in receiving benefits from your vitamins, or flushing them down the drain. cassette tape or CD (approx 1 hour in length) ……**.also just $9.95**

Dr. Vitko's Public Lecture Series – cassette or CD (Over 6 hours of thoughtful health knowledge delivered to a live audience.) Want to feel his enthusiasm for the subject? See why he is so excited about health! **$39.95**

4 Easy Ways To Order
Mail: **Use easy order form on the next page.**
Check/Money Order/MC/Visa
Internet: Order online - concretehealth.com
MC/Visa
Phone: Call Toll Free 1-877-418-3324
8 am to 5 pm EST (M-F) MC/Visa
Fax: Easy order form to 330-482-5225MC/Visa

Easy Order Form

Copy this form and mail to Rock Solid Health Solutions,
Inc. PO Box 5 Columbiana, Ohio 44408

		Tax
3 Weeks To Perfect Cholesterol (without drugs!)---Hardcover Book	**24.95**	*1.88*
Enjoy Incredible Health---Cassette or CD-----------approx. 1 hour	**9.95**	*0.75*
Supercharge Your Vitamins and Your Health--Cassette or CD--approx. 1 hour	**9.95**	*0.75*
Dr. David Vitko's Public Lecture Series-------------Cassette or CD---------over 6 hours (Live)	**39.95**	*3.00*
Subtotal		↑
Ohio residents only add 7.5% sales tax See individual product tax in right column.		*Ohio Residents*
Shipping and Handling within continental USA $4.00 first book, tape or CD/$2.00 each additional		*Sales Tax*
Total		

MasterCard and Visa Accepted

Card Number_____ Exp. Date _____

Signature_____

We also accept check or money order. All orders are shipped as soon as humanly possible. **Make check payable to: Rock Solid Health Solutions, Inc.**

Name_____

Address_____

City_____**State**_____

Zip Code_____

Phone_____

Optional:
If you would like to periodically receive information from Dr. Vitko regarding timely health topics and/or new products, please trust us with your e-mail address. We promise not to sell it, or share it with anyone else.

e-mail address_____

Did one of our customers refer you to us? If so, please provide their name so that we can show them our appreciation. They just paid us the highest compliment possible!
Referred by:_____

City_____State_____

Thank you for your order!
Look for other products as well as free health articles on Dr. Vitko's website: **concretehealth.com**

<u>Need a speaker with a passion for health?</u>

Dr. David M. Vitko not only studies health extensively, he lives what he teaches. He has made the change from a typical American with "seemingly good health" (actually poor health), to one who has experienced "rock solid health". That transformation has forever changed his outlook on health and life.

Through his lectures he brings this transformation into focus for others. His life experiences give him the unique ability to connect with the average person. He understands the daily struggles that make lifestyle and dietary changes difficult at best. Struggles with work, the kids, extended family, and even what we see or hear causes us to do things we know are not healthy. Stress often undermines efforts to achieve good health.

Couple this with the tremendous amount of misleading health information we are exposed to each day, and the odds of becoming healthy seem to be stacked against us.

Dr. Vitko knows that just because something has been repeated for decades, does not necessarily mean it is true. Do you really know the difference between misleading health information and that, which is absolutely *rock solid*?

It is often hard to tell the difference these days. How can you ever reach good health if you are not sure of the correct path to follow?

Poor health is most often a result of doing the same wrong things over and over. Dr. Vitko is the one speaker who helps his audience to clearly understand what those wrong things are, and how to correct them.

Few speakers can deliver this level of health knowledge in an understandable and enthusiastic way. Dr. Vitko accomplishes this, **and** provides his audience with the motivation to help them quickly make healthy changes that will last for years to come.

For more information call:
1-877-418-3324

Or write to:

Dr. David M. Vitko
at
Rock Solid Health Solutions, Inc.
P.O. Box 5
Columbiana, Ohio 44408